WE ARE ALL SELF-EMPLOYED

The biggest mistake you can make
is to believe that you work for
someone else.

*—H. Jackson Brown, The Father's
Book of Wisdom*

WE ARE ALL SELF-EMPLOYED

HOW TO TAKE CONTROL OF YOUR CAREER

Second Edition

Cliff Hakim

BERRETT-KOEHLER PUBLISHERS, INC.
San Francisco

Berrett-Koehler Publishers, Inc.
235 Montgomery Street. Suite 650
San Francisco, CA 94104-2916
Tel: 415-288-0260   Fax: 415-362-2512 www.bkconnection.com

ORDERING INFORMATION

Quantity sales. Special discounts are available on quantity purchases by corporations, associations, and others. For details, contact the "Special Sales Department" at the Berrett-Koehler address above.

Individual sales. Berrett-Koehler publications are available through most bookstores. They can also be ordered direct from Berrett-Koehler: Tel: (800) 929-2929; Fax (802) 864-7626.

Orders for college textbook/course adoption use. Please contact Berrett-Koehler: Tel: (800) 929-2929; Fax (802) 864-7626.

Orders by U.S. trade bookstores and wholesalers. Please contact Publishers Group West, 1700 Fourth Street, Berkeley, CA 94710. Tel: (510) 528-1444; Fax (510) 528-3444

Berrett-Koehler and BK logo are registered trademarks of Berrett-Koehler Publishers, Inc.

Printed in the United States of America

Berrrett-Koehler books are printed on long-lasting acid-free paper. When it is available, we choose paper that has been manufactured by environmentally responsible processes. These may include using trees grown in sustainable forests, incorporating recycled paper, minimizing chlorine in bleaching, or recycling the energy produced at the paper mill.

Library of Congress Cataloging-in-Publication Data
Hakim, Cliff, 1951–
    We are all self-employed : how to take control of your career / Cliff Hakim.
        p. cm.
    Includes bibliographical references and index.
    ISBN 1–575675-267-4
    1. Work-Psychology aspects. 2.Employee motivation. 3. Job satisfaction. 4. Self-Employed. 1. Title.

    HF5548.8.H23 2003
    650.1—dc21   2003050247

Second Edition
08 07 06 05 04 03   10 9 8 7 6 5 4 3 2 1

Book producer: Tolman Creek Design   *Copy Editor:* Laura Lionello
Indexer: Shan Young

TO AMY, for honoring and loving

TO GABRIELLA, for being,

TO MY MOTHER, for encouraging me to touch people;

TO MY FATHER, for showing me,

It's another day, make the most of it.

Contents

Preface

This book is not about starting your own business. On the other hand *it is*. Its intent is to challenge and influence your work beliefs—the ways you think about and do your work. "We are all self-employed" is an empowering belief that you can use to steer your direction and influence your quality of life. "We are all self-employed," whether you work in an organization—CEO, vice-president, manager, staff member—or outside an organization—consultant, supplier, entrepreneur. This might sound crazy at first but in today's world knowing yourself, collaborating with a team, and producing are more important than ever. Doing your job *and* going beyond it, beyond blind loyalty to any one organization or customer, is perhaps a new concept to some of you but it can reap enormous rewards—personally and professionally.

Individuals and organizations are undergoing constant and extraordinary change. People are losing their jobs, questioning their work-life choices, redefining their identities, consolidating their debt, simplifying their lifestyles, expanding their options, and shifting their loyalties. Organizations are laying off, doing more with fewer employees, building self-directed work teams, and buying services from a growing, contingent, part-time, workforce. Many workers, regardless of their level or industry, are learning that they must begin to think and act carefully and openly as they grow personally and the world restructures around them. The old "security" or foundation is gone.

People are looking for a new anchor, a "personal anchor," in a transformed marketplace. *We Are All Self-Employed* explores what it means to practice a self-employed attitude and how to make it work for you.

Thinking of yourself as self-employed is an attitude that says, "I am a business partner with integrity and a responsibility for working with the organization and the customer, and attending to my own personal and professional development." The idea—we are all self-employed—is the truth about us and a statement about our changing and challenging world of work. It is not a selfish truth but a liberating one—a philosophy for success and satisfaction.

This book is designed to allow you to be your best, authentic self and allow you to use your skills and aptitudes, express your values, and feel you are making a worthwhile contribution. I encourage you to be creative and to take action—to deepen and expand your way of thinking and pursuing your goals. *We Are All Self-Employed* supports your passion, purpose, and productivity. Together, these elements are your power and security in a less predictable, more competitive world. Understanding who you are and what you believe is the source from which your passion and purpose flow. Passion and purpose are your spirit—your deep interests and values—your inner core. From here spring ideas and the energy to commit to productivity—meaningful action. I hope this book will help you build the bridge between managing practical tasks like paying the bills and living your dreams.

Why This Revision?

I revised this book primarily to take people from merely surviving (adapting) to succeeding (creating). Surviving, continually making adjustments to a shifting culture, downsizing organization, or demanding customer can turn us into androids—robotic, unfulfilled, angry human beings who make mechanistic, routine changes simply to adapt to environmental conditions. You don't have to give up your uniqueness and the treasure chest of tools that you have for problem solving. Instead you can act courageously and contribute your ideas and actions rather than accepting others', and even mine, at face value.

Surviving = Adapting
Succeeding = Creating

In my practice as a career and executive counselor, I have worked with many professionals at all levels in the fields of sales and marketing, human resources, engineering, health care, teaching, finance, and others. I revised this book to reach a broad audience and support many of you who have already begun your journey to make sense of personal and global changes. As you reconcile and determine what strengths you bring—skills, values, purpose, passion—and what you want to bring, you will undoubtedly add value to your worklife, workplace, and a marketplace of dynamic change.

Since the First Edition

Since the original writing of *We Are All Self-Employed*, the world has aged 10 years. I have, too. Now more than ever I'm concerned and adamant about living life fully and want to urge you to do the same. At midlife mornings blend with and fold quickly into evenings, and 10 years—3,650 days—seems but a moment.

Since the original writing, it's been confirmed: employment is temporary, downsizing and restructuring are the norm, and guaranteed job security is dead. Dorothy, in *The Wizard of Oz*, captured the astonishment of many. She astutely noted, "My, people come and go so quickly here!"

These conditions leave a precarious void or, depending on your view, a vast and illuminating space for learning and possibility. If you choose challenge over capitulation, you'll take charge of your worklife and fill the void with new beliefs, behaviors, and what you want. In fact, in today's world, you are given one guarantee: You will eventually lose or leave your job, no matter how good your performance. The project you're working on will finish or the contract you signed up for will have a deadline—whether you do a good or a bad job—it will end. You'll become bored, your desire to grow will kick in, and you'll look to make a job or career change. Your full-time job, the one that seems so secure, will run its course or become obsolete. Change —individual, organizational, and societal—will continue, and increasingly will become your responsibility.

The purpose of revising *We Are All Self-Employed* is to further encourage you to face these issues, to adopt a more entrepreneurial and responsible attitude toward worklife.

This Book Asks

How will you take control of your time going beyond survival, to thrive—working and living, joyfully and productively? What choices will you make to further express who you are? How will you make the most of this moment? Will you let go of what no longer feels good to you? What will you add that feels better? Is what you're doing right now advancing you toward your goal? What are you waiting for before you act?

My Hope

My hope is that *We Are All Self-Employed* will give you the optimism needed during this time in your life to do your magic. I hope it will draw you closer to your heart's desires and guide you to become more conscious of the fact that the life you have and what you have to offer is a gift. In addition, I'd like this book to augment your courage as you pursue the unknown, explore possibilities, and move toward your goals. And as you form your own impression of a self-employed attitude, I encourage you to walk away with one thought, idea, or tool that guides and lightens your steps and clears and deepens your path.

Cliff Hakim, August 2003
Arlington, Massachusetts

Acknowledgements

This book is a manifestation of my personal worklife and beliefs. Ever since I was a child, my gut instincts have known that we are all self-employed, that none of us really works for anyone else. I am indebted to many people who, throughout my life, have participated in my learning and influenced my direction, and to those who have made this revision possible.

I thank my family. Thanks to Amy and Gabriella, for your loving tolerance during those times we'd talk about the school day or vacation plans and I'd be only half present with the next sentence swirling around in my brain. Amy, I have been blessed by your trust and ability to embrace uncertainty; I have felt and am fueled by your resolve. Gabriella, thank you for your question "When will your book be published?" The sparkle in your eyes when you asked kept me going.

Thank you to my friends: Bruce Albert, for your thoughts on learning and growing; Deborah Sosin, for your tears and perspective; and Ralph Katz, for your gut honesty and reflecting my energy.

Thank you to my colleagues: Mary Jacobsen, for seeing my light and helping it to shine brighter; Rene Petrin, for your supportive words, always, and expertise on mentoring; and Kim Cromwell, for your example of courage and your belief in my work.

I'm greatly indebted to the reviewers of the manuscript. Valerie Andrews, thank you for getting up and shouting; Irene Sitbon, thank you for your reminder that my message is a wake-up call to our souls;

Lisa McLeod, thank you for citing that "courage" is essential to work-life change; and Peter De Macarty, thank you for challenging me to examine the "real unfairness" of the workplace. I am blessed to know that you all appreciate my "energy and passion," and acknowledge the "dreadful import" of my message. I wrote a better book because of you.

At the foundation of producing this book were the purpose, passion, and productivity of the Berrett-Koehler team. I am grateful to Steven Piersanti, president of Berrett-Koehler Publishers. Thank you for recognizing that the timing was right for the rebirth of *We Are All Self-Employed* and for leading your independent team members in offering their interdependent bests to publish this second edition. The team included Maria Jesus Aguilo, senior manager, international sales and subsidiary rights; Patricia Anderson, vice president of business development and strategic alliances; Gail Caldwell, fulfillment manager; Marina Cook, sales and marketing associate; Michael Crowley, senior direct sales manager; Robin Donovan, senior online marketing and promotion manager; Kristen Frantz, director of sales and marketing; Brenda Frink, publicity and promotion associate; Jenny Hermann, business development and marketing associate; Catherine Lengronne, administrative assistant; Bob Liss, vice president, operations and administration; Ken Lupoff, publicity manager; Kate Piersanti, copyright editor; Mark Schoenrock, finance director; Jeevan Sivasubramaniam, managing editor; Kathy Slater, accounting manager; Richard Wilson, vice president for design and production; and Ginger Winters, senior human resources/office manager. Thank you for your out-of-the-box thinking that included me as a full partner.

Thank you to Jimmie Young from Tolman Creek Design for the design of this book and to Laura Lionello, editor, for adding clarity and panache.

My gratitude, beyond words, goes to my clients. It is each of your journeys that have humbled and fortified mine. I know their stories will give life to this book and encourage its readers to tell theirs and express their "self-employed" attitudes.

INTRODUCTION

Burning the Grass

Way back when, in the late summers or early falls, my grandfather would set his lawn on fire. We called it burning the grass, and he believed it fertilized the soil and made the lawn come back greener. The neighbors called it crazy and eventually the fire department put a stop to it. As a child of seven or eight, I was curious and sometimes confused. I wasn't sure whether to believe my grandfather or the neighbors. As the years passed I began to accept my grandfather's ritual as a means of producing something better. Even though others saw it as chaos, I learned that my grandfather knew what he was doing. The grass always felt thicker, a better surface for play!

What looks like chaos can actually be, and is often, a vital part of change and growth: learning a new profession, taking a new job, or starting a new company. The process requires moving through the chaos and darkness—the anxiety, confusion, resistance, and solitude—to eventually assemble the many disjointed, misunderstood, and often unrecognizable pieces. It is a time of reaching inward and learning about yourself. It is a time of reflection, faith, observation, idea generation, resolve, and reform. It is a time central to all those who examine their "employed" attitude and choose to learn or deepen their "self-employed" attitude.

As my grandfather burned the grass I learned not to judge what I saw even if others did. I stood back, watched, and appreciated that something was going on even though I didn't understand what. I knew that with patience and perspective I would notice something valuable. Now I look back at burning the grass as a metaphor for his life and possibly many of ours. My grandfather's message to me was this: Look back through the years; you can learn from them. You don't have to repeat them, but you can borrow from them. Pause, reflect, and understand what you want. Appreciate the process, then respect your wisdom—do what you think is right. You can make a difference.

If we are open to history, learning, and our own wisdom can be great teachers. Many of our forebears—farmers, poets and writers, and sales people—were "self-employed." They burned the grass: raising crops to feed a growing nation, writing prose to record our history, composing poetry to inspire innovation, and selling new products and services to shape our lifestyles. Workers eventually came to believe that those who owned their own companies were self-employed and those who worked for organizations were entitled to their job, benefits, and perks. They were not, however, self-employed. The urgent message of *We Are All Self-Employed* remains, and particularly of this second edition, is that the "employed" attitude no longer exists. A "self-employed" attitude has emerged as the central belief for fueling your worklife. Will you burn the grass, fight for and follow your path? Will you respect the organic nature of being and contributing yourself? Or, will you settle for Astro Turf? You're the boss.

Who's the Boss?

Over the past dozen years I have set myself free. I have recreated myself from executive search consultant to author, speaker, and career and executive counselor. During the 10 years I spent in executive search, I worked diligently carving out an organizational niche, developing a steady client base, and earning amply. But, I didn't like who I was becoming in this role and what I was doing on a daily basis. My spirit was too tightly packaged up—ossifying, locked into a stultifying routine. Although "search" was a means to learn about the business world, build relationships, and make money—all of which I am grateful—my heart was under-nourished and my hands were under-utilized. I longed to express my own beliefs and personality. I missed stretching and asserting my imagination, being unbound from decaying personal beliefs and constricting organizational rules. I missed putting my creativity to work for others.

Fortunately, I listened carefully. I heard the ping: a personal calling to self-leadership. Have you heard the ping? Ping...I think I'm dissatisfied, but I'm not sure. Ping...Work is okay, but maybe that's not good enough. Ping...People say the company won't look after my career, but I doubt that will happen here. Does the ping, as you scuttle about, come and go? What is your experience? Open your heart and listen. Does the ping fade while the message that you can take charge and do something that is more distinctively you in the world sounds? Doing who and what is you, I've learned, is the only sustainable work. It's impossible to follow the dreams and trends of others for very long. They are short lived.

The first step toward taking charge of your worklife is to know that the process begins with YOU. Shh. Hear the ping in your heart. You may expect an in-your-face awakening but rarely is there a sledge hammer bang. Usually the messenger is subtler. Ping!

At some point in their transitions, most of my clients ask, "If I follow my heart, how will I make money?" Using myself as an example, I respond, "I override my fear that I won't make much money writing by stimulating my heart. I ask myself, 'What do I love, even if I may not be the best at it? What do I most want to do—even if the learning curve is long, steep, and uncertain?' I sit with these questions and my answer usually emerges. 'Expressing myself and sharing my wisdom through writing, speaking, and counseling so that others can borrow my example and ideas to express themselves and trust and use their own wisdom is my passion.'" I can't ignore; I must respect and live my truth. My answer—a purposeful, spirited mantra—propels me forward in my life journey. And yet, as it is so for you, I know there are no guarantees: the writing of this book, a project, is temporary. And, ultimately, you the customer will judge its worth. Is there an answer—some relief from the natural churn of worklife and the common feelings—fear, anxiety, confusion—associated with change and risk? Yes, there is an answer. You can replace fear with the belief that you are the boss.

Who's the Boss? You Are.

I thought for too long that life should be easy. You may believe that life should be easy. For me, though, digesting this belief eventually led to indigestion. I'd begin a project, become impatient when the going got tough, and quit. Writing this book, for example, would have been impossible guided by my old life should be easy belief. "Life is difficult." That first sentence in Scott Peck's bestseller, *The Road Less Traveled*, was the catalyst that most reoriented my thinking. He continues, "Once we truly know that life is difficult—once we truly understand

and accept it—then life is no longer difficult. Because once it is accepted, the fact that life is difficult no longer matters." I first read these
words in 1978 and they continue to fortify my thoughts and guide my
actions today.

I know in my gut, after much personal and professional growth, a
decade of global flux, and developing my practice and nurturing a family, that I am fully responsible for my worklife. Of course, I'm not only
independent, attending solely to my heart's calling and choices. I'm
interdependent, too, collaborating with and contributing to others.
Combining the two, I am a self-leader—the onus, still, is on me to
imagine, plan, explore, and create the worklife that I want. In any
economy, I'm the boss of my worklife. You are, too, whether you work
inside or outside of an organization. Who's the boss? You are the boss.
You're in charge of your worklife. This is the message of this book.

You're the boss of discovering and acting on what's in your heart.
You're the boss of managing the feelings and tensions that naturally
arise when navigating uncharted territory. You're the boss, knowing
that you will sometimes clash with your tired belief that someone else
is the boss. You're the boss, making the choice to struggle and go
beyond your struggle to a "self-employed" attitude. And, you're the
boss—the one in charge—of asking for support, or asking to be left
alone, when risking change.

If someone pointed the finger at me and said, "You're the boss of
your worklife" I might be skeptical, possibly scared, and a bit excited.
Right now, you might be experiencing one, or all three, of these feelings. If you are, bear with me. You need not make your I-am-the-boss
decision now. All I ask is for your curiosity, that you question your
"employed" attitude and remain open to summoning and shaping your
"self-employed" attitude.

Why Read This Book?

To self-lead:

understand and do what is in your heart,

overcome your fear of change,

reawaken and free your spirit,

and become more productive than ever.

Read this book if you are interested in feeling healthier at work and in your life. Without a clear sense of self, working with others lacks health, conviction, and joy.

Read this book if you want to inspire your children. Frequently, Gabriella, my eight-year-old, asks, "Dad, will you tell me about your work? What do you say to your clients? What are you writing now...the same book?" She and her peers discuss what their parents do and Gabriella wants to be ready to share with her friends. She also wants to learn how I handle what may one day be in store for her when she enters the workplace. Gabriella and her friends are learning ways to use their ideas, skills, heart, and energy to become productive, to promote and manage change, and to enjoy their work.

Read this book if you want to live a fuller life and feel good about every stage while continuing to contribute to the lives of others.

What's New

This revision emanates from my soul. I've updated *We Are All Self-Employed* because I know I'm the boss. I know that you're the boss, too. The economy, job marketplace, and our zeal for personal growth are constant reminders. What's new in this edition includes a refined Worklife Creed; many fresh, supportive, and diverse, worklife examples; stimulating and thoughtful quotations; an emphasis on the freedom and vitality of the heart—purpose and passion in worklife; and a Who's the Boss? Check-In section, consisting of five summary and thought/action questions at the end of the first six chapters. On page 162 you'll find the Ten Commandments for Winning Interviews. The last chapter shares several meaningful-work steps, plus an inspiring meaningful-work interview.

How This Book is Organized

The first chapter of this book assumes that you have some familiarity with, and in some instances that you have experienced the virtues of, the "self-employed" attitude. To refresh, there's a comparison between an "employed" and a "self-employed" attitude on page 13. The comparison presents and clarifies the minimum critical requirements for you to develop, deepen, and/or sustain a self-employed attitude. Individually, the subsequent six chapters form the essential dynamic building blocks for assimilating and constructing a "self-employed" attitude. Collectively, they are a powerful transformational system for living this attitude. The checklists and exercises in each chapter will deepen your understanding of a "self-employed" attitude. Starting on page 14 the chapters are united into six beliefs that constitute a worklife creed.

Even though I've used the widely accepted term "career" in the subtitle (How to Take Control of Your Career), throughout *We Are All Self-Employed* I'll generously use the term "worklife" instead. This is because, in conversations with my clients, they share work and life issues and dreams. In addition, as you mature, healthy work and career decisions can only be made when you consider and integrate other aspects of life: relationship, children, parents, housing, education, recreation, community, world and financial affairs, health and longevity, and your spirit.

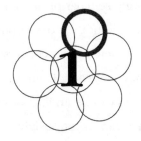

DEEPEN YOUR "SELF-EMPLOYED" ATTITUDE

Ready yourself for a new era

Congratulations for coming this far. You have found a personal anchor rather than relying on external moorings. You have confirmed in your heart and mind that blind loyalty—someone else will take care of me—is dead. You have struggled with old beliefs and have updated your loyalty to "conscious" loyalty or a self-employed attitude. Yes, full responsibility for your worklife is only proper, not selfish, in our unpredictable and demanding world.

Are you ready to deepen your "self-employed" attitude? Reflect for a moment about a time when you felt forced or coerced into making a change. Did you actually change? Or, did you wait until no one was looking and then fall back into a familiar pattern? What price did you and your organization pay for this misalignment: Lost time? Disgruntled customers? Low morale? I promise that I won't make you, in any way, adopt a "self-employed" attitude. Instead, you can feel and explore your readiness.

Whether I'm delivering a seminar on rethinking work or talking one on one with an individual about their development, I repeatedly notice that people go beyond the intellectual conversation to actually engage in renewal only when they are ready. Even for the most conscious, recognizing personal readiness can be an illusive challenge. Fear, crowded schedules, and impatience can thwart insight into your needs and your best intentions. I've heard clients say, for example, "I don't know what happened. In the past three or four years my company has changed, but I haven't!" The following is a list of questions that have emerged from my counseling practice. You can use them to assess, measure, and affirm your readiness. If you check three or more, you likely are ready to learn more about and create your self-employed attitude.

Personal Readiness Questions

Do you want to...

- make more worthwhile contributions?
- take charge of your attitude?
- reawaken your spirit?
- fully express your passion?
- overcome your work fears?
- stay in your current job and grow there?
- take control of your worklife?
- better align with customers' needs?
- maintain a clear sense of self while you work with others?
- establish a new work attitude?
- set a leadership example?
- approach work with grace?
- inspire others?

Consider your answers to these questions. Change exists everywhere—inside and outside of you—and there is never a perfect time to learn and grow. I'll bet that you've already experienced the value of a self-employed attitude. And, and if you've read this far, you're ready or getting ready to advance your attitude.

When Steve Piersanti, President of Berrett-Koehler Publishers, called me to ask if I'd consider a revision of *We Are All Self-Employed*, he said, "Two years ago you never gave me an answer." I paused and asked, "An answer to what?" "Two years ago," Steve responded, "I asked if you'd like to update *We Are All Self-Employed*. It's still a great title, and the market is hungrier than ever for the concept. You've already sold thousands of copies." I responded, "Back then I wasn't ready. Let me think about this for a few weeks and I promise I'll get back to you."

It took me just a few days to respond. My "yes" was aided by three of the Personal Readiness Questions listed above: Do you want to make more worthwhile contributions? Do you want to reawaken your spirit? Do you want to set a leadership example?

I answered Steve with this e-mail:

Your call to me was timely. After rolling around some thoughts and searching my heart, I'm ready to commit to a revision of *We Are All Self-Employed*. Several people, including yourself, have said that the concept is more alive today than ever. Increasingly, my clients are accepting this belief as their truth and are showing their willingness and ability to take greater responsibility for their work-life. In addition, when I mention the concept more casually, at a party or school event, people nod as if to say, 'Of course, we are all self-employed!'

How You Work and Live

Whatever your work situation or career stage—company worker, business owner, part-time worker, unchallenged worker, laid-off worker, or new worker—this book shows you how to manifest a "self-employed" attitude. The following comparison highlights the minimum requirements for and distinguishes between the "employed" and "self-employed" attitudes. Attitude implies that each of us has the ability to learn and make choices about how we work and live. If you choose to live a self-employed attitude you will feel shaky at times, maneuvering through past and present internal obstacles and external barriers. However, your diligence and curiosity will lead you to inner security, your goals, and the opportunity to contribute the best parts of yourself in an unpredictable, formidable world.

Separately, the six self-employed beliefs are the individual subjects of each chapter; each is talked about and illustrated in detail. Collectively they form a strong spine, supple and supportive, for leaving the mindset of dependence—the black hole—behind. Like the human spine, if one vertebra is out of alignment we feel pain and our posture suffers. As you read this book, you will refer to the six "self-employed" beliefs at different times and make it your goal to work toward their ultimate alignment—the you're-the-boss attitude. The following chart compares the practical applications of the employed and self-employed attitudes.

"Employed" Attitude	Practical Application	"Self-Employed" Attitude	Practical Application
My employer or customers should change in ways that will benefit me. They are to blame if things don't work out.	My boss is all wrong. My customers don't know what is good for them. They'll eventually see things as I do.	I will begin the process of change with myself. Worklife development/ management is my responsibility.	With a career counselor's help I am able to assess my strengths and focus on my work priorities.
If I just put my head down and work harder I'll be safe. I can ignore my fears of knowing myself, losing my job, or understanding my passion.	After all I've done for them, they can't fire me.	I will face the dragon—my work fears—and replace it with passion. I will share my ideas; identify my skills, values, and desires; and ask questions to clarify my focus both for myself and my company.	I'll talk with trusted colleagues to clarify company goals and determine where best to focus my energy.
I am dependent on the company/ customer. They know my skills and what is best for me. They will take care of *me*.	Whatever job offer I get, I'll take.	I will integrate independence and interdependence. I will strive to be myself and collaborate with and contribute to others.	When I interview, I'll present what I have to offer, ask about what they need, and assess if the job is a good partnership for me.
I am enmeshed with the company/ customer. I work for them. Whether I agree or not, I do what is expected of me.	I sit attentively listening to what my boss or the group needs and do it.	I will join, not work for, my organization and customers. I provide a service based on equality and competence, whether I work in or outside the organization.	In a meeting, I listen and contribute my thoughts.
I can hold on to my successes and be satisfied. If I can only get what I want —position, title, benefits—then I can rest on my past accomplishments.	I know the politics enough to stay safe.	I will commit to continuous learning, personal growth, and gaining new per- spectives. My career is a lifetime endeavor. My mistakes and successes lead to expanded thinking and further contribution.	I ask questions to determine my customers' needs and make the necessary adjustments in our service.

continued

"Employed" Attitude	Practical Application	"Self-Employed" Attitude	Practical Application
What I do doesn't really matter. This is just a job. I bring my body to work and leave my spirit behind.	My job is boring; there is nothing new to learn.	I will create meaningful work. I am resourceful and able to give value to my work—market my skills and negotiate for my needs—and make a contribution regardless of my job or level.	I ask questions, take in feedback, sell my ideas, and try to meet a tangible goal when possible.

The following pages explore why the six beliefs that comprise a self-employed attitude are critical to your worklife.

1. I Will Begin the Process of Change with Myself

In the past, the company cocoon provided a secure place with income, benefits, title, advancement, identity, and stability. The cocoon protected the workers' identity while they waited for retirement or even for death.

It's a new era. Now you must follow your own worklife path. How? Step out of line. When I was 12 years old, I took a trip with my family to Scarsdale, New York to visit my friend, Mark, and his family. An exciting part of our stay included a train ride into New York City. It was a weekday. All the passengers at the station seemed so serious. I listened for laughter, looked for a smile. The year was 1963. The majority of people boarding the train were men dressed in dark suits and white shirts. "Penguins," I thought! Each held a briefcase in one hand, with a paper, probably the Wall Street Journal, tucked underneath that arm. When the conductor shouted "ALLLL aboard" I watched wide-eyed. Each was lined up, dressed alike, carried the same paper, and marched past me onto the train. This depressing image of my possible future has stuck with me for almost four decades. Was this what I had to look forward to for my worklife? Was I expected to be the same as everyone else? I grew up in a home where individuality was fostered. My grandfather burned the grass, tilling the land and buying and selling real estate. My father, too, burned the grass as he mapped out his own strategy and carved out his sales territory. He worked at a large insurance company and said, "They never had to manage me. I focused on my goals and saw every day as one of opportunity. I earned more than the branch manager!" Now I have more words for my childhood experience. Many of these men worked for large corporations. "Corporate" beings! They had a dress code and an unspoken employee/employer agreement: Produce for us and we will guarantee you a job. Furthermore, remain loyal and we will take care of your career.

A whole different world later and people are still lined up. These people may not be wearing dark suits, but colleagues, acquaintances, and clients—men and women—have all lamented their narrow and shallow paths. They have said, "I'm bored with what I do" or "What I do pays the bills, but I'm unhappy. Work takes so much out of my hide!" or "I envy my sister—she loves her work. Somehow, she had the courage to use her aptitudes. Instead, I did what my parents expected of me." In each situation, these people are stuck—lonely, frustrated, and restless. They are marching to someone else's drummer, not their own.

Accepting the idea that we are all self-employed changes the way we view our entire lives. "It's very scary to me sometimes. It takes time to assimilate," says Jean, director of an external research program at a computer manufacturer. "Eighty percent of the time I say I want to take command. For the other 20 percent, I'm still scared. Everybody has got to come to the point of being their own change agent."

Expecting that your employer and customers will continue to change is realistic, but expecting that they will change in ways that will benefit you is not. Identifying and mastering your own strengths—your skills, values, purpose, passion, and aptitudes—increases your control over your job productivity and career mobility regardless of external circumstances. The dependent mindset—that is, hoping others will change and then blaming them for what doesn't work for you—gives others your power and leaves you stuck in unsatisfying situations.

And the day came when the risk it took to remain tight inside the bud was more painful than the risk it took to blossom.

—Anais Nin

2. I Will Face the Dragon—My Work Fears

At a Harvard University sponsored lecture by the Association for Part-Time Workers, guest speaker Dr. Harris Sussman, strategic consultant, opened by saying, "We are all self-employed." He reported that the fastest-growing group of workers consists of people working from home. These people, who work at all levels of diverse occupations—accounting, real estate management, financial planning, sales, and publishing—are connected to other individuals and organizations via telephone, fax, and e-mail. In 1987, Charles Handy wrote, "By some estimates, one-quarter of the working population will be working from home by the end of the century. From home is different than at home. The home is a base, not a prison." The end of the century has passed and Mr. Handy's prediction is here. In my own neighborhood, Elles the graphic designer works part-time from home and part-time at a television station. Ben the musician works part-time from home. The rest of the time he's on stage. And Josh the programmer visits his clients to assess their needs and brings his work home, too. Sally is a program manager for a large company. She visits the home office once every two weeks to meet with her team and customers. Via e-mail and tele-phone she stays connected with her staff.

We live in an era of necessary and multiple work alternatives—full-time, part-time, job sharing, and telecommuting. If you tend to be afraid because times have changed and will continue to change, it will be harder for you to see the virtue of alternatives and to take action. The majority of clients I've seen over the past years are working differently today. Generally, they overcame their fears of change through self-examination and deliberate, incremental action. As it is with most change, what is initially foreign and chaotic becomes accepted and routine down the road. Rarely did they know where they were headed; still, they delved into what was purposeful to them and, step by step, replaced fear with meaningful results. Ken, senior executive with a consumer goods manufacturer, said, "I had no interest in becoming a corporate executive. I got my MBA anyway 20 years ago. I recall, feeling desperate to do something with my life. I talked to no one about my choice…only observed my father. Now, thinking about following my heart is both exciting and VERY frightening, but I don't have a choice. I know I can be happier. I owe this to myself, and my children." Meg, a marketing manager, overcomes her fear by keeping her "ultimate goal" in mind, "to find a new job that allows the greatest expression of myself and my talents, where fun happily coexists with accomplishment."

Change can liberate people from situations—positions and titles—that no longer work or benefit them or others. The clients mentioned above overcame their central fear: If they let go of what they know, they would land in a permanent, cavernous void. Freed from their title and willing and able to grapple with their fears and fixed expectations, they tapped into their personal resources and sought work that fit their own growth and organization/customer needs.

3. I Will Integrate Independence and Interdependence

This book is a result of both a combination of my thoughts and a compilation of reactions, responses, and stories that I gathered in person or by telephone from working people across the United States—people from the dot-com bust, educational institutions, large corporations, small businesses, and nonprofit associations. When I talked with people about the notion that we are all self-employed, I was thrilled to discover the numbers of people who reacted positively. Some said, "That's it!" A few said, "Imagine if more people throughout the world could learn to think this way." One responded, "I can't imagine not taking control of my life. There's no security anymore. Being dependent is death." Another commented, "Your concept is in sync with these times." My question obviously and invariably evoked a visceral reaction. Although some didn't have all the words to explain their response, most understood that we are all self-employed. They wanted to continue the conversation, know more, and hear what others had to say.

I began each interview by asking, "When I say, 'We are all self-employed,' what does this mean to you?" Most often, the initial response was "Responsibility." Curiosity led to inquiry. I then asked, "What does responsibility mean?" The word responsibility captures the central theme of this book. It is the ability to act independently and interdependently—to be your authentic self (purposeful and passionate), collaborate with others, and work productively. We live in a world where self-leadership—taking responsibility for knowing yourself and for engaging in deliberate and constructive thought and contribution—is increasingly a core virtue. It is a choice to go beyond survival to success and satisfaction in worklife. Dependence is a succumbing to your fears. It will always hold you back from reaching your potential. Celia, a teacher in transition, said, "A while back I had an operation on my thyroid. For three or four days others took care of me—a necessity for a while, and a seductive one at that. Then I realized that I needed to take responsibility by not letting health concerns become an excuse for not living." Layoffs, unchallenging work, demotion, and personal challenges are part of worklife. They won't go away if you simply bury them.

4. I Will Work *With*, Not Work For, My Organization and Customers

Over the past decade many of my clients moved from one dot-com driven job to the next. Several were swept into the tidal fervor—naming their price and getting it. They profited. But many, those I knew and didn't know, did not. Today, economic buoyancy is deflated. Now you are called to "partner" differently, to think and act collaboratively and in terms of working with others. You, the individual, must distinguish yourself by knowing your heart—what you are passionate about—and how your passion can add unmistakable value to the customer. Clamping on to the latest trend will not offer you security or eradicate your fear. Trends are not permanent solutions, but temporary way stations. Selling and using your skills alone is not enough either.

Ann, a designer, partners with her colleague and network of vendors to beautify her customers' homes at a reasonable price. My wife, Amy, and I hired Ann to redesign our dining room. Initially, we focused on replacing the rug and buying chairs. Regarding the chairs, we explained, "Ideally, they would have a cushioned high back and seat, thin silhouette, and a narrow wooden ridge that horizontally framed the top of the chair. The legs would gracefully curve." Ann listened, not once debunking our wish, and said she'd scout the antique market and let us know what she found in a month or so. Four weeks later, Ann left a message: "I found your chairs at Antiques on Cambridge Street. Check them out and let me know what you think." I walked into the shop, spotted the eight chairs, and without sitting in them, sought out the dealer Burt and said, "Sold." We chose fabric and Ann's upholsterer re-stuffed and re-covered the chairs. After seeing the finished chairs, I called Anne and said, "Is there such a thing as too perfect?"

Ann partnered with us doing what she loves. She didn't follow some cookie cutter recipe, but listened to our request, honored our taste, and applied her expertise. If Ann had a working "for" us mentality, I don't think she would have been as confident and free to simply tell us that we'd find our chairs at Antiques on Cambridge Street. Friends had referred her to us and we have passed Ann's name on to others. Customers are lined up to work with Ann, despite the intrepid economy.

Workers in more traditional environments also face the working "with" or "for" decisions. A large Boston law firm voted and made the wrenching decision to close its doors. Founded in the late 19th century, the firm could not be saved by its historical roots. In the best interest of their clients, the firm was dissolved in a responsible and dignified manner. Over two hundred lawyers and other employees worked for the firm. Now each would need to take stock of their personal strengths and make decisions about realigning to work with a changed job market.

As individuals and organizations are forced to reinvent themselves, so is society. Individuals are now without guarantees of "expected" job safety nets—benefits, bonuses, and promotions. Organizations have always been loyal to there own survival and success. Are you loyal to your own survival and success? Will you work with or for others? Like Ann, will you see yourself with purpose and act with the confidence to deliver?

Realistically, we temporarily supply our expertise to an organization and its customers. Engineers are ad hoc to the organization, too, whether or not they see it or believe it, by supplying their expertise in the development of state-of-the-art technology. They will have work for as long as the organization needs them or for as long as they feel their work is suited to them. Nurses, in a similar way, are ad hoc to the health care facilities in which they work. They, as well, will have work for as long as the organization needs them or for as long as their needs are being met. This arrangement has its price, but if you choose to move to another organization—customer—you too will be ad hoc to the new organization.

None of us can afford to return to a closed mentality, to parental, hierarchical thinking. Trusting our leaders, wholly, can be unwise. Not only may your immediate job be at stake, but your savings and/or retirement could suffer as well. Instead, there is opportunity to take control of your worklife. It can be daunting, but extraordinarily rewarding, and no more painful than seeing your job and your savings circle a drainpipe.

5. I Will Commit to Continuous Learning

We all work two jobs—one of them is being our own worklife self-leader. Continuous learning is the central qualification of this job. Why continuous learning? Learning is your fuel for developing hope, insights, perspectives, solutions, and actions.

How can anyone work two jobs? One is demanding enough. Note the following job description. Like any job description, this one is fluid and may change as you and your organization or workplace changes. At the moment, try not to decide whether you would apply for or accept this job. First, simply read the description.

Job Description
Worklife, Inc.

Job: Worklife Self-Leader

Hours: An ongoing thought process and way of being; between two and four hours per week

Location: Flexible—at an office or at home, in your car, on the beach, at your favorite coffee shop, or as you walk to your next destination

Process: Self-paced

Summary: You must be able to take responsibility for your own career mobility and job productivity while making a contribution to the organization, customers, and the larger whole.

Primary Qualifications: Any worker at any level and from any profession can apply for this job. We encourage inquiries and your application at any time. We anticipate a continuous flow of openings, whatever economic conditions exist. The worklife self-leader position primarily requires that you take the initiative for working with others, career planning, negotiating with management for self-development needs, and recognizing ways in which you can add value to the organization and/or customer.

You must be able to:

- describe how things have changed in the marketplace, in your place of work, and in your job.

- discuss your concerns about loss, transition, and managing change.

- assess your individual responsibility and how much you can control in your job, with your customers, and in your organization.

- ≣ discuss the benefits of moving in multiple directions, not just up the ladder.

- ≣ feel good and confident about asking and getting the support you need.

- ≣ clarify and prioritize your values to then pinpoint the essential one.

- ≣ break down the artificial barriers between your jobs to see and harness the passion buried beneath have-to-dos, fear, and compliance.

- ≣ identify your skills and decide which are most meaningful to you and which are most marketable to others.

- ≣ develop action/results statements and learn how to use them effectively.

- ≣ examine your beliefs and determine which are barriers to growth and which are catalysts.

- ≣ develop one to three specific career goals and a professional and flexible development plan that includes a pliable timeline for meeting goals.

Salary: This is a permanent growth position. You may, or may not, earn approximately the same amount that you currently earn. Your earnings will fluctuate depending on your profession, your ability to negotiate, your workplace, and the marketplace conditions. Whether or not you decide to take this job, it is wise that you save as much money as possible and invest wisely in order to build a financial cushion for sustaining, renewing, and enhancing your worklife.

Philosophical Statement: You're the boss. We are all self-employed—inside and outside of organizations.

Values Statement: Working in our changing world requires authenticity—passion and purpose—collaboration, and productivity. We must know ourselves as individuals who are emotionally, intellectually, and spiritually distinct from our "employed" identity. With this self-knowledge, we can better identify our needs and values, build a sense of mission into our worklives, and contribute more to others.

Many of you are working very hard, trying to keep up with your job or lack of one, as well as meeting family, social, and community obligations. To take on the job of worklife self-leader along with your other responsibilities may seem unrealistic. Yet, this new job is a growing, flexible, evolving commitment, not another straightjacket that restricts you to rigid hours and routines. The description is a message and guide to encourage you to take part in the learning process of who you are and the changes and opportunities in your workplace and the marketplace. You and others who take on this job will most likely rewrite the description as you grow and as external conditions warrant.

6. I Will Create Meaningful Work

As a boy, I worked landscaping yards and painting houses. I worked in the glorious outdoors. I made my own schedule, found my own customers (some found me), and made my own decisions. My general goal was to improve and maintain property and develop my techniques. My commitment was quality—doing the best possible to satisfy my customers. Thus, I consciously gave meaning to my work. The more meaning I gave it, the more I felt thankful to have it. I embraced with deliberate thought and action what appeared routine to others. I learned, for example, to select the right paint or plants for particular conditions. My self-employed attitude was taking shape back then. No matter what stage of worklife, creating meaningful work develops over the years, increasing wisdom, self-esteem, and enthusiasm; attracting customers and rewards; and presenting new opportunities.

Judy, a director, cleaned houses before she joined a corporation. She reminded me, "As a director, my title and role seemed so different than my house-cleaning days. But essentially, I brought the same spirit and values. To each, I was present, worked toward efficiency, made something better, respected and supported people, and enjoyed earning results. I brought my spirit to a home and to the organization."

No work inherently possesses meaning. You develop a self-employed attitude by using your power to give meaning to your work. Only you can give meaning to your work and only you can take it away. Deliberate thought and action create a gateway to sustaining meaning in work. No matter what you do, creating this gateway and using your creative resources to develop meaning in your work is up to you. Even in the supposedly high-status professions—medicine, law, accounting—the rumblings of change are turning into large noises. "I saw medicine very traditionally. You open up an office or join a group practice and someone else takes care of billing, paperwork, and marketing," remarked Andy, an internist. "This is no longer true," he continued. "Today you must master business skills, including supervising others, computer proficiency, as well as your medical skills. One has an opportunity to gain control of one's employment destiny, leading to greater creative control and ideas. But one has to ride out social, economic, and psychological waves in order to keep one's head above water. All of a sudden you are thrust into the business world (whole world). We must overcome our resistance and master new thinking and skills." For many, overcoming resistance and mastering new thinking and skills is the entrance to meaningful work.

We Are All Self-Employed
A Worklife Creed

I will begin the process of change with myself.
Start with my own personal growth

I will face the dragon—my work fears.
Replace fear with passion and purpose

I will integrate independence and interdependence.
Be myself and collaborate with, and contribute to, others

I will work with, not work for, my organization and customers.
Do work and build relationships based on respect, equality, and competence

I will commit to continuous learning.
View my worklife as an ongoing journey

I will create meaningful work.
Work and live, believing that the world needs you and that you can make a contribution

Who's the Boss?

Check-In: Deepen Your "Self-Employed" Attitude

At the end of each chapter you'll find a Who's the Boss? Check-In like this one. The questions summarize each chapter contents and provide an opportunity for you to garner self-leadership: personal reflection, observation, planning, and action. If you and a colleague or friend is reading this book together, discuss your insights, explore and support each other's ideas, then actively plan for and engage in next steps. You'll intensify your independence—knowing yourself—and animate your interdependence—collaborating with and contributing to each other—a core tenant of the self-employed attitude (see Chapter Four, Integrating Independence and Interdependence).

Please remember that every question is an opportunity for understanding self, others, and the world. It's not for judging, censoring, or faulting.

1. What changes have you seen and/or experienced in the world that have influenced you?

2. What are some signs that you are ready to deepen your "self-employed" attitude? Was there an event in your worklife that marked your shift from an "employed" to a "self-employed" attitude—taking control of your worklife?

3. Can you recall a time or two that you've been in chaos— overwhelmed or distraught—and found direction, a new question, or fresh possibly?

4. What have you done to reinvent yourself in the past five to
   seven years? What valuable lessons might you borrow from
   these experiences to build your confidence, innovate—put your
   creativity to work—and reinvent yourself?

5. After reading the job description on page 22, what qualifications do you possess to take on the job of worklife
   self-leader?

BEGINNING THE PROCESS OF CHANGE WITH YOURSELF

Start with your own personal growth

EMPLOYED ATTITUDE

Dependent Mindset

My employer or customers will change in ways that will benefit me; they are to blame if things don't work out.

SELF-EMPLOYED ATTITUDE

Independent and Interdependent Mindset

I will begin the process of change with myself; worklife self-leadership is my responsibility.

Honor your Picasso. You are unique.

No one else on this planet is exactly like you. Because you've heard these words plenty of times before it's easy to deflect or gloss over them. Stop for a moment. Inhale these words: No one else on this planet is exactly like you. Let them swirl around in your brain and sink into your heart. I've written these words for you—they can make or break your fortune. Your uniqueness is invaluable if you are open, hungry, and obstinate enough to honor it—see it, hold onto it, and use it.

When I was a child, my mother said to me,
'If you become a soldier, you'll be a general.
If you become a monk, you'll end up as the pope.
Instead, I became a painter and wound up as Picasso.
—Pablo Picasso

Picasso struggled to know himself and observed how he got things done. He practiced, refining and valuing his talent. He noticed and innovated, discovering new forms of expression during his days and throughout his life: he varied his brush strokes, transformed paintings, and later adorned ceramic forms. He confronted and overcame his fears and positioned himself to make significant contributions—hundreds of now priceless paintings, sculptures, and artifacts. He didn't lay out his life in a predictable pattern, expecting perfection. He risked—no clear plan in sight. Each period of Picasso's life gave birth to another as he honored—learned about and used—his uniqueness.

Are You Ready to Listen?

"I'm finally ready to listen," Donald said. "After 10 years of trading stocks, I'm ready to hear that I've been using only part of myself as

I've interacted, mostly, with a computer screen. Trading, although challenging and intriguing, has segregated me from the people and some of the special ways that I can be helpful to them. My wake up call was a hearing loss. It stunned me. After a MRI exam, the doctor diagnosed that I had a tumor growing in my ear! My first question was, 'Will I die?' Fortunately the tumor was benign. I had two choices: have it removed surgically or vigilantly pay attention to my health and happiness to see if it would disappear organically. I choose the organic route. I have come to believe that many physical difficulties are metaphors for spiritual blocks and psychological concerns."

Donald continued, "The tumor grew, pressing against nerves which created a deafening reaction. The physical anomaly was a message telling me that I wasn't listening to others or to myself. I knew that I was unhappy sitting behind a computer terminal, but I was afraid and didn't know how to change. People would tell me, 'What makes you unique is your rich understanding of economics and your ability to teach others how to manage their finances. You can help— teach and counsel—people to see the bigger picture and to manage their portfolios better.'"

Donald finally heard the message of his uniqueness. His last MRI revealed that his condition had improved and he continues to advance in his worklife with the hopes that as he becomes truer to himself the tumor will shrink more.

Donald is not alone. Many people's worth evades them. For example, they say, "I have soft skills—listening, facilitating, problem solving. What are they worth?" One implication is seeing yourself as common, like so many others. People fail to see that their skills are only part of them. You truly are unique, just like Picasso and Donald.

Try this. Take a trip to a crowded area, a busy mall, or a bustling street corner. Step back. Does anyone look or act exactly the same as you? Ask yourself the following questions:

Does anyone in this crowd, listen exactly like me?

Does anyone in this crowd, talk or gesture just like me?

Does anyone in the crowd, appear to problem solve precisely like me?

Now, take the time to write down two or three examples that illustrate your unique ability to listen, communicate, or problem solve. When I do this exercise with my clients, they begin to relax, to see, and to accept their unique selves. After they finish their list of examples, I ask, "Would you endorse the page?"

When an admirer asked Picasso for his signature, he answered, "Sure. That will cost you thirty thousand."

Everybody's special.
—Mr. Rogers

The Simplest Gestures

Stephanie walked into a jewelry store during her vacation to New York City. The day was steamy, in the ninety-degree range. Her real intention was to take a break from the heat. As she peered through one of the cases, a salesperson approached and asked, "May I offer you a glass of water?" In disbelief, Stephanie replied, "Oh, thank you, but that's not necessary." A few minutes later, the young man reappeared with a fluted glass filled with crystal clear, chilled water. Balancing the refreshment on a silver tray, he approached Stephanie again and asked, "May I offer you a seat?" This time, Stephanie accepted his offer. She sat down and enjoyed every sip of her water.

What I found interesting was not only Stephanie's story, but also the order in which she told it. During her four-day trip, she visited famous sites such as the Guggenheim Museum, Saint Patrick's Cathedral, and Tavern on the Green. A simple glass of water may appear insignificant when compared to such special places. Yet Stephanie shared the water story first. Stephanie commented, "I hope this young man is aware of his uniqueness. I can only imagine the string of his repeat customers."

Declare Your Studio

Where do you go to find and honor your uniqueness—to hear your deepest thoughts and become open to possible answers? Sometimes an inanimate object—a tree—or a place where you feel comfortable—the beach or a chair—can become your private studio. The artist Randal gathers ideas from the outside world, walking through the woods, hiking around a pond, watching a butterfly, or listening to his students, and returns to his studio to reflect on his experience. He holds his studio as a private space for examining what he believes, for opening his being to new thoughts and possibilities, and creating what he loves.

You may be thinking, "Well of course, artists have to have studios. That's where they work." For many artists this is so. But I contend, not all artists use their space for renewal; some use it only to produce. And if the studio is only for production, at some point it will become a factory: A workplace that churns out product or replicates service. The marketplace, and our personal will to grow, continues to push and pull at all of us. To avoid extinction or go beyond survival to thrive, the artist or the factory manager must enter his or her "studio"—examine process, break routines, and reshape behavior—to refresh the self and rejuvenate the system.

Imagine for a moment, you, the artist. You are one, you know. You want to do your art—repairing engines, programming software, decorating homes, inventing natural solutions for human health—and express, through your work, your unique self. To do so, and to let go of decaying forms and to take on new thoughts and behavior, a studio is necessary.

Sonia, an information center manager said, "I rarely talk with others at work about my career. We're too busy. At other times, I'm not in the mood to go public with my concerns. I'm kind of a private person." After we talked further Sonia said, "My job involves handling huge amounts of information and dealing with people's problems. Twenty-two people are on my staff. At the end of the day, and sometimes during, I need to get away from the information overload and, frankly, the people."

Although Sonia had a core position within the company, she questioned "Do I feel committed to my work?" Approaching her mid-thirties, she was becoming more interested in attending to other parts of her life. Sonia felt it was the right time to sort out whether to stay the current course or embark on a different one.

I asked, "What have you done to sort out where you want to head?" Sonia said, "Our corporate headquarters is located near a beautiful park. I would walk through the park whenever the weather was nice enough. I happened upon a special tree—it is old and has an unusual shape, jutted and angular. The exposed roots are gnarled and the trunk is solid. Sometimes I'd put my hands on it. Somehow, the rough feel of the bark helped me to feel grounded. Mostly I would talk to the tree."

"What would you say?" I asked. "Well, this might sound odd," replied Sonia, "but I would ask the tree to give me clarity, direction, and motivation. I looked to the tree for hope." I asked, "What were you hoping for?" "Enough courage," said Sonia, "to discover what I really wanted from my work. It was not enough for me to be successful in others' eyes, I wanted to feel good about my work too."

Sonia continued, "I started visiting the tree last October; all its leaves had fallen. Now that it was springtime, many of the surrounding trees were blossoming, but my favorite tree had no leaves. I was afraid that it was dead. Because of my work schedule, two-weeks passed before I revisited my tree. When I saw it, I couldn't believe my eyes. My tree—it was alive! The leaves were full and flourishing. Like me, it was a late bloomer or maybe just different!"

"In my work environment, people labeled successful were those who advanced to management. I realized I'm different and I need to recognize my difference. I'm really not cut out to manage people. I may be okay at it, but I don't enjoy it. I want to be happier—more fulfilled—in all parts of my life."

"How will you bloom?" I asked. Sonia replied, "It is never too late. I have decided to take a risk and respect my difference—'demote' myself to senior information consultant, a staff position in which I would advise internal and external clients. I wouldn't manage people. It wouldn't be a demotion but a promotion to what I really want. My schedule would become more flexible and I would directly add value to clients."

Sonia befriended a tree, found her courage and direction, and negotiated with her boss to make the transition from manager to consultant. She has created a path to the rest of her life, too.

Change Begins at Home

On a trip to Nantucket, a quaint Cape Cod island off the coast of Massachusetts, I met Josh, a world traveler. Josh had been to the Near and Far East, Africa, Europe, South America, and a variety of islands. As he was telling me about his journeys, he pointed past a knoll and proclaimed, "Over there, that's the house I grew up in." I said, "You've returned home?" I'll always remember Josh's response. "I tried to find the answers outside of me. Traveling taught me that change begins at home."

Living a self-employed attitude begins at home—with you. Insight—knowing yourself—and deliberate hard work—planning and action—are the basis of personal change and inner security. Josh traveled the world seeking an answer; his question was, "What do I want to do for work?" "I realized," Josh said, "traveling didn't give me the answer. In retrospect, traveling was part of my answer. The other, more significant, part was an internal journey—the adventure of knowing myself—coming back home." Through soul-searching, courage, perseverance, and his knowledge of the world, Josh found his answer: adventure. And he has since become a foreign diplomat.

I asked Josh what he would recommend to others who decide to embark on a journey of personal growth and discovery. He offered five basic suggestions:

1. Remind and encourage yourself, continuously, that you can change and feel better and more productive in your life.

2. Take time every week to think about what you are doing and learning. If you are so inclined, keep a journal.

3. Find people to talk with—a friend, spouse, counselor, or support group—about your feelings, concerns, and aspirations.

4. At least every three or four months, take a look at your goals and ask yourself, "What do I need to learn to achieve them?" Develop a flexible plan and take action.

5. View confusion and fear as normal parts of your growth. Working through them takes courage—vulnerability and bravery—and will lead to clarity and success.

The following chart gives an overview of the work world today and builds on what Josh has to say by suggesting some guidelines to consider as you navigate toward a self-employed attitude.

The Changing Work World

The Work World	You, as Self-Employed
Organizations and the marketplace have changed and will continue to change.	You must change too.
Financial and extrinsic rewards are important, yet ephemeral.	Balance internal and external success.
Blind loyalty is defunct. The worker-organization contract has changed.	Know and be loyal to yourself.
Hiring is a rigorous process.	See yourself as a partner: discover what the workplace needs and decide what you want to give to it.
Climbing the corporate ladder isn't sustainable—there are many more options.	Redefine yourself, create work, and explore personally satisfying niches.
The market is customer-and productivity-driven.	Find joy in your work and know how you can add value.
Organizations have become flatter and leaner.	Develop *in* your job. Climbing the ladder is only one option.
Full-time employment has become only one form of work.	Part-time work, consulting, job sharing, and working *from* home are viable options.
Workplaces are redeveloping, task-oriented, learning environments.	Personally develop and grow, affirm your purpose and passion, and contribute.

Personal Renewal

Personal renewal is the harnessing of your creativity, abilities, beliefs, thoughts, and actions in order to rethink, redefine, reconstruct, and refresh your worklife and achieve fulfillment and productivity. In my work with individuals, both inside and outside of organizations, it has become clear that as organizations renew the way they work, individuals—as was true of Sonia and Josh—become more responsible for learning the concepts and tools for creating, utilizing, and managing change.

People are taking more control of their worklives—stepping forward and out. Rita, a marketing specialist, was given an exit package when the organization for which she had worked for 10 years was stalled for growth and desperate to survive. Within a few months, she landed a similar job in a corporate environment. Two years later, I received this New Year's update from her:

> The accelerating and intensifying pace and expectations of the corporation have exceeded my desire. So, this time, I'm actually feeling pretty good about leaving and excited about reinventing my career. I am pursuing three things: marketing consultation for small businesses, project work for ad agencies, and college-level teaching. I may change my mind, but I really don't think I want to rejoin corporate ranks.

Personal renewal is a gradual, endogenous process that requires ongoing growth from the inside of you outward. The Merriam-Webster Dictionary says renewal is "to begin again; to revive." Personal renewal involves curiosity—discovering—and patience—rediscovering—your personal knowledge. Courage is also vital, as is the willingness to experiment with and apply what you learn in order to strengthen and use your power.

I want to beg you, as much as I can, to be patient toward all that
is unsolved in your heart and to try to love the questions
themselves like locked rooms and like books that are written in
a very foreign tongue. Do not now seek the answers, which
cannot be given you because you would not be able to live them.
And the point is, to live everything. Live the questions now.
Perhaps you will then gradually, without noticing it, live along
some distant day into the answer. Resolve to be always
beginning—to be a beginner!
—Rainer Maria Rilke

Achieving results through personal redeveloping can be complex and confusing. The process is rarely linear. There was a time when achieving and advancing in one's work seemed more straightforward and certain accomplishments all but guaranteed particular results. Teachers graduated with their master's degree and headed directly for an opening in a public school; new MBAs were recruited by and had a choice of working at several Wall Street investment banks; a diligent supervisor could expect to be promoted to manager. External conditions aligned, clearing paths for relatively unfettered career advancement and recognition.

To ease the pain, reduce complexity, and streamline the personal renewal process, I ask individuals to focus on the four questions that follow. You can apply these same four questions to realize and harness your power, whether or not you work in or outside an organization or are in a worklife transition.

1. What do you *really* want?

Do you want to bake bread or sell houses? Do you want to act in plays or write scripts? Do you want to use your persuasive abilities to practice law or raise funds? Do you want to have the latitude to think big?

Do you want to design computer technology or consult with customers on how to use the latest technology, or both? Do you want to become part of a core business or start your own? Really is emphasized because I want individuals to search their histories and question others' experiences to make soulful, heartfelt choices. You can do something expertly, for example, organize files or refinish furniture, but I am suggesting that you go to your studio—be patient and have courage—and ask yourself: Do I really want to pursue either? Why burrow deeply and ask yourself this question? Because you become your choices, and because you only live once. Your life is special. Live it now.

2. What do you want *less* of in your worklife?

Do you want less doubt? Do you want less fear? Do you want less anger? Do you want less direction from and reliance on your manager? Do you want less of a commute? The less of question is important to ask yourself because it gives you some understanding about what you must let go of, potentially opening a clearing and maximizing your energy to pursue what you really want.

To this question Becky, a former teacher said, "I treasure the experiences I had with my students and revel in the communication we continue to share. However, *I did not feel personally or professionally challenged and inspired.* This feeling was at the crux of my decision to leave teaching. Teaching required of me more than it offered me. Fortunately, this is not the case for many teachers, for the work surely offers many of them personal and professional rewards."

Becky continued, "I want less of my time to be consumed by working early mornings to late nights. When teaching, I felt like I had no life. I disliked the rhythm of the teaching work schedule—I felt out of sync with the rest of the world—up at 5:00 a.m., in bed at 9:00 p.m. I want to feel less stagnant and old—in the classroom all day by myself, then home all night correcting papers or creating lesson plans, by myself—Yuck!"

Admitting and sharing what Becky wanted less of focused her energy toward what she wanted. She said, "I want to take a good look at what has driven me—fear and insecurity—and what drives me now in my career pursuit. I want to move beyond reactionary behavior, to a more healthy, fluid, process of career decision making."

3. What do you have to bring to others?

What strengths—purpose, passion, skills, values, ideas, and personal qualities—do you offer? How can you derive personal satisfaction and success as you bring these parts of yourself to your work? Why battle your weaknesses? You don't have the time. Shift your focus to utilizing your strengths—qualities that more accurately and easily define who you are—and joys—those pursuits for which you have genuine enthusiasm.

To this question Peter, a photographer, said, "At the start of my recent journey I did not jump; I was pushed. Nearly three years ago I left a secure but intensely discouraging job as a manager in a large company to take a chance on an Internet-related business. It failed, as so many others did. I was laid off and for the first time in more than 25 years, I found myself with no place to go when I got up in the morning. I was confused, fearful, and depressed—all the normal emotions for the process I was forced to go through. I tried hard everyday to look at this time as an opportunity, a chance to make an even better worklife, but the confusion and discouragement often got the better of me. I openly wished I had not been presented with such an 'opportunity.'

"But time away from the standard workday did provide inspiration and a changed vantage point. I realized that I had become disconnected from my core values and the first love I had in work: photography. Thinking I should stretch myself, I had given up what gave me most satisfaction. Perhaps for some, the need to get out of a 'comfort zone' is a necessity for challenge and growth. For me, getting out of the comfort zone had succeeded only in making me uncomfortable. My epiphany came on the golf course, another passion. Prior to this point, whenever someone I met asked me what I did for work, I went into a long, unsatisfying rap about my recent job and layoff. One glorious morning, a new playing partner asked me what I did for work, and I just blurted out, 'I'm a photographer.' I said it without thinking, surprising myself with my own clarity. For a photographer is who I am: not an editor/administrator/internet entrepreneur, but a photographer. From that point on, it was as clear as it could be to return to what I loved and did best: capturing images that tell stories. It is my passion, and the need to reconnect to it had become irresistible."

4. What will others buy?

Is what you want to do worth a purchase price? How do you benefit others? Why would your company or a customer pay you for what you do or sell?

Peter answered the question, What do I have to bring? Next he answered the question, What will others buy? He said, "After working with a talented web designer, I discovered my site was a powerful expression of who I am and what I do for my customers. The result was that the majority of my successful leads came through my site: people I had not met or talked to, who were not referred to me, but found me strictly on the strength of the photographs and writing on my site." Toward the end of Peter's first year of business his calendar was booked. His customers wanted—paid for—what he wanted!

These questions work best when you ask, "Who's the boss?" and respond, "I'm in charge of my worklife." As you take charge, you might want to consider the questions as a constellation, akin to a group of stars; their grouping, not one alone, creates the design. These questions can guide you toward creating a new career opportunity for yourself as you answer them and put them into action. But because things don't always work the way that we think they will, let the questions sit. Don't rush to answer. Often when my clients are looking for a worklife change and they come up with their first potential job option—an answer—I say, "Good first step. Now let's look at why you think this might fit and at other possibilities." Together, we sit back, generate new ideas, and evaluate what we have. The best answer(s) will emerge through a combination of examination and serendipity.

Streamlining Personal Renewal
1. What do I really want?
2. What do I want less of in my worklife?
3. What do I have to bring to others?
4. What will others buy?

Wild Horses

Rollo May says, "There are, in the unconscious, a number of horses straining at the bit to be off in different directions." I frequently say to clients, "Your work is to harness the wild horses—personal qualities, skills, values, feelings—running around inside of you so that you can lead with your beliefs, manage change, align your resources, and progress toward your goal." Naming and harnessing the wild horses is a metaphor for personal renewal. The questions (What do you really want? What do you want less of in your worklife? What do you bring? What will others buy?) are your guides, the harnesses.

Realigning the Wild Horses

Lisa was multitalented but unfulfilled. Over the span of her worklife, she had worked in the areas of counseling, teaching, proposal writing, public relations, drama, and administration. When Lisa sought consultation on career and work issues, she was an editor in a large publishing firm. She was also at a point of desperation, feeling that her work fundamentally had little meaning or interest. Time was passing her by, and she complained, "I have done so many things and done them well, but I've never been happy at any of my jobs. I don't know where I'm headed."

Together, we explored the range of her feelings—fear, anger, hopelessness—and identified other obstacles to her finding career satisfaction. I asked Lisa to clarify her skills and other strengths using a particular tool called Harness Your Wild Horses. She used this tool as a vivid metaphor to develop a self-employed attitude and achieve her worklife goals. First, she listed all her positive personal and professional qualities and how she wanted to use them in a work setting. Her list included thoughtfulness, curiosity, creativity, and empathy. During the course of several sessions, I helped Lisa identify her skills: writing, creating, analyzing, and synthesizing. I encouraged her to imagine that each of her skills represented a wild horse that was confined within a fenced-in area. What would happen if the gate were just opened? All the wild horses would scatter in different directions. But, what if each of these horses was harnessed? Their energy would be focused and they would be free to move forward productively and joyfully.

Lisa's team of wild horses was now metaphorically harnessed. This technique effectively helped her to move forward in reality. She unearthed a longtime goal of being a scriptwriter and, over a period of four months, with occasional coaching sessions for guidance and encouragement, launched a job search with renewed energy and a positive outlook.

The question remained, Could she get paid in this role? Her inner harnessing created energy that led to a focused networking effort. She discovered a scriptwriting position in her company's video department, where she now works.

Reframing as a Harnessing Tool

Reframing transforms meaning and behavior. A rock becomes a paperweight—you place it rather than throw it. The piece of fruit becomes decorative art—you notice its contour but refrain from taking a bite. A puddle you jumped over becomes a mirror you now look into. Your impatience becomes your desire to achieve. You step back, clarify your goal, and focus your energies. Eric, a set designer, for example, has enjoyed traveling the world as he has teamed up with others to create the backdrops for movies. Now approaching his late 30s, although he has enjoyed and friends have envied his exotic life, he's ready to trade the movie set for setting a different stage in his own life: marriage, home, children, and work that still is creative but requires less travel.

You can reframe thinking of yourself as employed to thinking of yourself as self-employed. Rather than quitting your job or blaming your manager because things aren't just so, assess how you might change and alter your behavior. I overheard this conversation between Harry and Anna at a party:

Harry: I've been in this job for over a year. I don't think I'm in the right one. The pace crawls and people don't seem very motivated.

Anna: You said the same thing about your past job. If I recall, you lasted about a year in that one too. I'll bet if you leave this one, the same will happen in the next. You'll get discouraged, blame others, and leave.

Harry: What do you mean? This is a coincidence.

Anna: It's time for you to own up to your situation. That coincidence stuff lets you off the hook and gives someone else your power. I have another friend who's been divorced twice in the past seven years. She says the solution is another husband. I don't think so! She's got to take some responsibility…look at her own behavior before making another choice. Otherwise, she'll repeat the same pattern. I'm thinking there are some similarities between your work dilemma and my other friend's marital travails. Knowing you, I'm sure you could hunker down and think of ways to bring gusto to your work and workplace.

If Harry listens to Anna and takes responsibility for his choices, I'm convinced that he'll be able to reframe blaming and escaping into learning and growing. He could change his behavior right where he is to not only survive, but also to thrive.

After expressing anger and grief over her demotion, one client, Andrea, reframed her situation as a time to learn as much as she could about herself and her work options. She wrote a note to me: "The time of job loss is painful but also very precious in the sense that it allows/forces people to discover." As Andrea learned about herself and her career options, she got to the point of seeing her boss as a catalyst and felt that she would never have discovered these other dimensions if she had remained in the same job. Demotion, in her eyes, became a promotion. Lisa, the editor, reframed her background. She harnessed her wild horses and focused her energy to become a scriptwriter. Both Andrea and Lisa thought about things differently and discovered a means to create new possibilities in their lives.

Reframing "Career"

"Career defined me," proclaimed Mara, a city planner. "City planner—that's who I was. No matter what, snowstorm or sick child, I'd go to work. Now, some years later, I've learned there are other parts of me; my job is only one part." Richard, an engineer and professor said, "Career for me is to be productive—an inherent need to solve problems and be productive." And Toby, a consultant, commented, "I don't think in terms of career but in terms of my skills. My job is applying my skills to a company's or client's needs."

Career, for some people, is what defines them; for others it is an active state; and for many it has meant and will continue to mean following a specific course or an occupation, such as a career in law or engineering. As you grow and the reality of your worklife and the workplace shifts, reframing can be an invaluable tool, but only if the new point of view you're adopting feels genuine—zestful—to you. Career could mean a subtle but potent shift to worklife consciousness: choosing a variety of jobs or projects during your lifetime in which you utilize your evolving skills and values and deepen your aptitudes and interests to create work and life harmony, adventure, and contribution.

For me, career is a vital evolution of self-expression and an opportunity to contribute to others. Feeling good about and challenged by the process—the steps I take to learn and achieve results—is crucial to me. If I didn't enjoy grappling with ideas and words and wasn't compelled to add ongoing value to you, I would not have revised this book.

View continuous learning—not perfection—as the goal of work.

—Mary H. Jacobsen, Hand-Me-Down Dreams

Reframing Your Career Mobility

The following examples show how some of my clients have reframed
their behavior to achieve their career goals.

Current Situation *What's Going on Now*	Reframe *New Viewpoint*
I'm arrogant	I'm self-confident
I'm impatient	I like to get things done.
I'm a poor leader	I'm an excellent individual contributor and team player
I have difficulty closing off options.	I'm flexible. I ask others to help with the final decision.
I'm too aggressive	I'm determined.
My skills are too specific.	I'm a problem solver and fast learner. As the company changes, I can contribute and adapt.
I feel discouraged	I need a rest
I'll take any job	I can focus and chose from three possible options.
I've been told I'll never make the switch from nonprofit to profit or manufacturing to service.	This change may not happen in one move. Instead, I'll make my move incrementally—on a project or part-time basis.
I'm "job searching."	I'm "partnering" with others.

There is No One to Blame

Blame has no place in the process of personal redeveloping. Blaming the boss for not getting a promotion, blaming the customer for not buying the product, or blaming the competitive job market for not getting the job will hold you back from learning what you need to learn to progress to your next goal. Blame creates judgment that interferes with learning and growth. You stay stuck. One client, Tye, a 46-year-old investment analyst, hoped for years that his firm would recognize his ability to work effectively with customers and reward him appropriately. It never happened. Fed up, he left the firm, blaming its managers for their lack of attention and recognition. Shortly thereafter, he returned to school to study counseling psychology. Now Tye laments, "I've wasted time and money. School feels like an unreal world to me and I miss the business world. I can't believe I made such a poor decision at my age."

Before he left his job, Tye believed the firm would change in ways that would benefit him. When he decided to go to school, he grabbed the first opportunity that would satisfy his need to be in a people-oriented profession. In both situations Tye blamed others for his unhappiness, lack of insight, and inability to represent himself. With some counseling and coaching, Tye realized that he could have built on his experience at the firm and sold himself into a position that allowed him to more fully use his abilities and explore his interests.

Don't Blame, Reframe

After a six-year period at the same hospital, Roberta, a pediatrician, inadvertently discovered that her salary was much lower than that of her colleagues. She was angry and her initial reaction was to call me and say, "I've been treated unfairly and I need to start looking for a job elsewhere. I don't think I'll be able to get a raise. Would you help me plan a job search?" After evaluating her options, Roberta began to see that she might experience the same inequity at another facility. Then what would she do?

She told me she was afraid of being rejected if she asked for a salary increase. I encouraged her to talk about her fear and, as she did, she discovered that her plan for immediate action was precipitous. A better plan would involve using one of her best skills—research—to uncover information about what other physicians were earning in similar situations, in and outside the hospital, before she acted. In addition, to reaffirm her abilities and contributions, she took an inventory of her skills and accomplishments. (This process will be discussed later.) Researching what others were earning, taking an inventory of her skills and accomplishments, and organizing her thoughts helped Roberta view her current situation more clearly. Informed now, not driven by anger or fear, she could enter into negotiations with increased self-confidence.

Roberta made an important strategic and philosophical decision: She reframed, looked at her situation as if she were self-employed. She did her research and clarified her value to the hospital. She scheduled an appointment with the manager of her unit to "discuss an important business matter." Prior to the meeting, we role-played possible scenarios. In the actual meeting, she presented her case calmly, offered her research for review, and, after a period of negotiation, received a salary increase.

Up is Not the Only Way: Reframing the Career Ladder

Question: How does a career ladder fit into transforming organizations?

Answer: For the majority, it doesn't.

Latitude is necessary in transforming organizations. People need to make decisions flexibly, move to where problems need to be solved, and get the work done. When organizational growth appeared boundless, the system took responsibility for the workers' upward mobility, pushing them up to the ladder's next rung. As organizations grew, workers learned to expect advancement: The organization would take care of them. Today's flatter and leaner organizations can no longer support hundreds of people climbing their career ladders and motivate workers in the traditional fashion. This is the new reality—the career lattice.

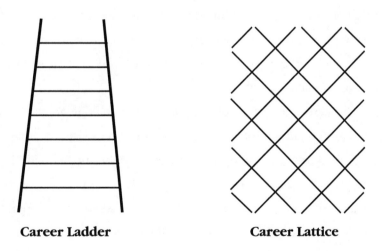

Career Ladder   **Career Lattice**

A career ladder suggests that there are only three ways to go: up, down, or falling off. Up usually means success. Going down or falling off...well, most of us try to avoid these. By contrast, a career lattice is a viable alternative for career mobility and job productivity for its structure supports different paths, each one involving career choices based on skills, values, interests, competition, workplace and customer needs, and individual and group initiative. A career lattice provides many options that a career ladder cannot. Douglas, for example, worked his way up the ladder to become a partner in a public relations firm. As partner, his role changed from direct consulting with clients to managing workers. But as the marketplace changed, he needed to lay off staff and step off the ladder. Douglas became a consultant again, moving in any direction—that is, using the lattice—so that customers would be served and the firm would succeed.

Career ladder thinking brainwashes us to compete with others for more pay, prestige, visibility, and fewer jobs up the ladder. Competing alone can divert us from focusing on our jobs. On the other hand, the career lattice, as Douglas discovered, affords different ways to think and act, thereby increasing opportunity and opening passageways for contribution. Career lattice thinking helps us concentrate on excelling at our work and delivering service. These are necessary tools for competing in the marketplace and for discovering work that is personally and organizationally valued.

The career lattice would support a junior engineer in his or her efforts to contribute to a project without the person necessarily moving "up" into another position. Rather than being rewarded with a title—which typically has little to do with performance in a dynamic culture—the person would instead be rewarded with the opportunity to contribute and learn, with the possibility of earning more money by meeting mutually defined goals.

For a senior engineer, the career lattice would encourage her or him to mentor a junior worker and gain knowledge of new systems design and customer needs. The rewards could include recognition for developing others' potential, financial remuneration (compensation aligned with the flatter, leaner system), and the learning of new, marketable skills. When appropriate, both junior- and senior-level engineers could also be encouraged to rewrite their job descriptions and create new job titles. These changes would more accurately account for and reflect their growth and the needs of the organization and the customer.

Career-Ladder Thinking	*Career-Lattice Thinking*
Movement is restricted—up or down.	Movement is flexible—up, down, and from side to side.
Promotions rule. Titles are revered.	What and how workers contribute are most important.
The system is autocratic—the boss has the answers.	The system is collaborative—"let's see what we can figure out."
Short-term strategy—temporary thinking and activity.	Fluid, long-term strategy—"we encourage you to grow and hopefully, with us."
Expertise is horded at the top of the ladder.	Expertise is utilized companywide.
Rewards are based on loyalty and title.	Rewards are based on learning, contribution, and performance.
Much internal competition with others exists, sometimes at the expense of the organization and customers.	External factors are considered, and competitive goals are set by the worker.
Workers are dependent on others for self-worth.	Independence, flexibility, and teamwork are fostered

Career-ladder thinking—positioning workers for upward advancement—makes less and less sense. The cornerstone of lattice thinking is self-leadership, encouraging employees to take control of their own careers. Career-lattice thinking means creating a shared vision that embraces career mobility for the individual and a competitive advantage for the organization.

This diagram represents the traditional career ladder in an organization. Compare it with the career lattice diagram that follows.

Career Ladder

Vice-president of engineering (one)

Manager of engineering (one of two)

Senior engineering product manager (one of nine)

Engineering project manager (one of seventeen)

Associate engineer (one of twenty-five)

Junior engineer (one of fifty)

Career Ladder: Up is the *only* way to advance.

Career Lattice

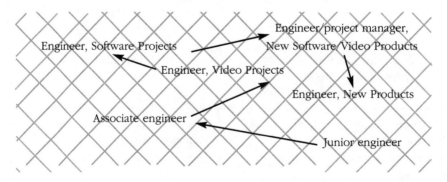

Engineer/project manager, New Software/Video Products

Engineer, Software Projects

Engineer, Video Projects

Engineer, New Products

Associate engineer

Junior engineer

Multiple Roles
(Engineer, Software Products)

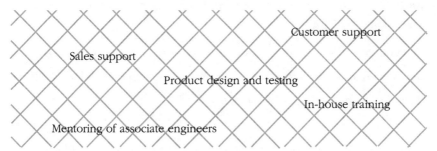

Sales support

Customer support

Product design and testing

In-house training

Mentoring of associate engineers

Career Lattice: Job mobility and multiple roles are possible for more workers.

A False Security

The linear path of climbing the career ladder represents a false security. Climbing the tidy ladder may have been effective when organizational growth seemed boundless. But as organizations continue to flatten, thousands of career ladders have been built and then collapsed. There is no longer the need, pageantry, or wealth to sustain them. Instead, defy career ladder thinking and give your worklife a boost. For example, go to the Internet—a mega-viable worldwide career lattice. With a few keystrokes, you can survey multiple sites, learn about options, save time, and get relevant information that a senior librarian, executive, or banker might have, or may never have, provided.

The Career Lattice at Work

Brandon, an in-house attorney for a financial service firm, said, "I'm planning to retire in three years. I guess surviving is enough until then." "Say more," I said. "I'll survive, keep my job if I continue to do what the company wants from me. Essentially, for 20 years, this is most of what I've done." During my initial meeting with Brandon, I counted that he had used the word "surviving" eight times. Six-feet, four-inches tall, Brandon walked hunched over, a survivor bordering on a victim, posture.

As the company readied itself to meet new customer demands Brandon's boss asked him to make a job change, which would include some different responsibilities but actually lead to a demotion. To properly negotiate his options, Brandon needed to talk through his frustrations and evaluate his situation. I became Brandon's coach. I said, "To survive, you will not need me. You are already surviving. My interest is to help you turn the corner toward thriving—making personal and dignified decisions about what you really want even when there's no clear goal in sight. This will require that you first take control of your career by deciding what is most important to you in life now." Although "control of his career" was a foreign concept, Brandon was enough intrigued and uncomfortable to experiment.

As Brandon reviewed his worklife history with me, three significant areas of life interest emerged: 1) Leisure—including family, friends, sports, and travel; 2) Ministry—involving church and giving back to the community; and 3) Work—contributing to the management and customers of the firm. In the meantime, Susan, his boss, proposed three primary new job responsibilities for him, including marketing, mentoring new recruits, and legal administration. When Susan met with Brandon and shared her proposal, Brandon said, "I'll think it over." This was Brandon's stall tactic, a means to mask his despair and depression and buy time to think through other possibilities.

I asked Brandon, "What did you need to think over?" He said, "I thought about all those people who perished September 11th...they all had hopes and dreams...cut off in a moment. Life is short, surviving only isn't good enough. If I accepted Susan's proposal, I'd place myself in her control and further depress myself. Also, I'm still unclear about what I want and about what my proposal is to Susan and the firm."

I said, "Brandon, this is a positive sign, a significant step toward taking control of your career. For a moment, let's depart from looking at specific job content to evaluating what you want now in your life."

On the left-hand side of a flip chart, I drew three circles representing Brandon's present life. After viewing and talking about this illustration, I asked Brandon if he would diagram what he wanted his life to look like in the near future.

Brandon's Life Circles

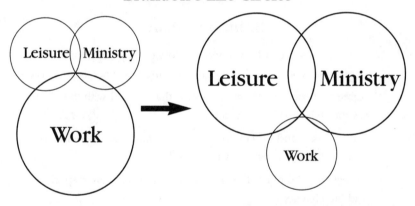

In the surviving mode, Brandon's work circle clearly dominated. It was approximately twice the size of the leisure and ministry categories. Brandon said, "When I compare the diagrams, I realize that I have been living my life in the reverse of how I'd like it to be. In my heart, I want to shrink my work responsibilities and expand my involvement in leisure and ministry. My leisure is fishing, golf, gardening, and spending time with my grandchildren. And ministry is volunteering at the church and running a summer camp. I've been focusing on holding on to work as the dominant area in my life because I haven't known how to make the transition from surviving to thriving."

Brandon's realization was the key that opened the gate for him to walk his own path. I asked Brandon what he specifically would change to get him into a thriving mode. He wanted to work a flexible four-day week, stay involved in legal administration, groom his replacement, and take on a marketing role focused on retaining customers. Brandon could utilize his history with the firm as an asset for coaching others. When I pushed Brandon for a fourth idea, he said, "I'd like to start up a formal career development program within the firm and give to others in a similar way in which you have [given] to me."

To move forward with managing his career, Brandon developed this plan:

Brandon's Plan

- ≡ Reassure Susan that he wanted to add value by developing a negotiable work plan that would meet the firm's needs and his own.
- ≡ Agree to a compensation adjustment that aligned with the responsibilities of his new job.
- ≡ Thank Susan and his cohort for their support and discretion as he worked through what he wanted to do.
- ≡ Be patient with himself as he transitioned to his new responsibilities and life change.
- ≡ Ask for support and involve others in his transition including, Susan, his wife, and other members of the executive committee.

Brandon continues to work with his firm, but in a new role. On his way toward early retirement, he is thriving—contributing to his colleagues, customers, and a younger generation of workers—and feeling fulfilled in his daily involvement.

Seeing Your Freedom

Our new era playing field is chaotic and complex. It forces some workers into unwelcome expanded roles and others into positions where they have a job but feel deskilled. Others, though, are seeing the freedom; that is, they are choosing new roles and new ways of working. Paul, a marketing director with a food-products manufacturer, saw the staff whittled to a bare minimum. He had to redefine his role as a staff consultant, becoming once again a valued player in an evolving organization. He took the initiative to analyze the market and reassess his skills. He rearranged how he used his skills so they matched what he wanted to do and met the needs of division managers and customers. Another client, Laura, an accountant, was initially laid off because the real estate firm for which she worked was gobbled up by a larger firm. As she mourned her loss, she also recognized an opportunity for herself. Laura negotiated an interim accounting position by convincing her employers that she could ensure a more even transition. At the same time, she explored other options and planned her future. Ultimately, she decided to start her own accounting service for small businesses. Her first client is her former employer. In the past, employers would have avoided such arrangements with ex-workers.

Paul and Laura both realized that it's a new era. They each looked at what they needed to do to change. Another type of playing field exists—one with fewer bosses, one that is hungry for new ideas and solutions, and one in which by knowing yourself and seeing opportunity you can reapply for a new job or invent one! Today, the market is much more willing—even eager—to do business with you. But first, you must see the freedom, committing to the journey of rebirth as you experiment and explore to find alternatives that express your passion. This new era, our economy does not need another follower; it needs your passion and your determination to make contributions to others.

Do You Think it's too Late?

Mona, a 30-something administrator, asked, "Do you think it's too late for me? My passion is math and I think I'd like to become a math teacher." I responded, "What do you think?" "Well," she said, "though my undergraduate degree is in anthropology, I have always been a natural at math. I've been here, in the same administrative job, for nine years. I can't believe I've had this one job for so long. When I take a look at myself, I'm concerned that my life is going by and that I'm not doing what I love to do. I'm considering going back to school to get a math degree or a teaching certificate."

As our conversation unfolded, I assured Mona that she was on the right track to assess her life and to note what is missing. I said, "Remember to recognize and give yourself credit for what you bring— skills, aptitude, and experience—to your goal of becoming a math teacher. Your wisdom and strengths tip the scale in a positive direction, and it so happens the job market is aligned with your goal. School systems need qualified and inspired teachers, especially in the math area!"

I received the following note from Mona eight months later:

It has been a 'little bit' of a long road but I am very pleased that I am officially a high school math teacher. I finished the seven-week summer Institute for New Teachers program, handed in my portfolio, and passed all needed certification tests.

I am also happy to announce that I have accepted a fulltime teaching position starting this September. I will be teaching math to freshmen, sophomores, and juniors and I'm very excited about the school. The school is in the next town over from where I live—only a fifteen-minute commute!

Thanks for all your support and words of encouragement. It looks like my journey was all worthwhile.

Go Beyond the Ordinary, Do Your Magic

Mark Levy, my friend, founder of Levy Innovation, and the author of *Accidental Genius: Revolutionize Your Thinking Through Private Writing,* is irreverent about expressing his magic and how he helps others find and use their own magic.

I asked Mark, "What is your personal magic? Can you give us an example of how it works for you?" Mark responded, "What you generously call 'my personal magic' others might call 'my mental illness.' But, sure, I'll talk about it. First, let me define it.

I interpret 'my personal magic,' as meaning the curious perspective and spark I bring to projects. And if that's your meaning, I agree. I have magic. Of course, one of the reasons I have it is because I'm a magician, a genuine, pick-a-card magician.

When you're a magician, you look at the world in odd ways, as if reality is pliable. Take, for instance, this paper coffee cup on my desk. Now a layman barely notices this cup. But to a magician, the cup is not only something to be noticed, it's to be scrutinized and deconstructed. I look at this cup and see its recessed base. Why is that important? I could hide a coin under there, and magically produce it at an opportune time. What about the substance inside the cup? Most people would assume it's coffee. A magician takes that assumption and plays with it. What if it were actually sand? Or mercury? Or spiders? How could the magician not just fool you but also astound and entertain you by exploiting your default thinking?

Magic is about delighting people by twisting their perceptions, and that's a key element in making a business successful, too. So, the approach I take to inventing a trick, I apply to business.

When I wrote *Accidental Genius,* I wanted to publicize it in a big way. The problem? It's a book about using private writing as a problem-solving tool: nothing implicitly dramatic about that. So how could I make people want to know more about it?

I issued a news release with the headline, 'Man Prepares to Stop Midtown Traffic with His Mind,' and that's what I did. I sat with my laptop for four hours in the window of the country's largest bookstore, the Barnes & Noble across from Lincoln Center, in New York City and used my freestyle writing techniques to solve problems. Each time I typed a sentence it would appear on a screen mounted against the window, so people could read what I was thinking. At times, hundreds of people blocked the street to read my messages. The upshot of the stunt? I got on CNN Financial Network and the bookstore, which usually sells two copies of a book, has sold close to 800 copies of *Accidental Genius*. So, while I didn't perform a standard trick, I used all the elements of stage illusion to create delight in the audience by twisting their perception as to how thinking and writing are supposed to happen."

Maybe Mark's magic will give you permission to recognize and experiment with your own personal magic, whatever it is.

Expectation versus Reality

One of the common challenges that many people face in their attempt to do their magic is focusing on their expectations versus the reality. Expectation refers to what you anticipate will happen as a result of your efforts, hopes, and societal standards. Jesse, an architect and designer, has established a design firm in Boston over the past 17 years. He has learned that his magic is rooted in his unusual ability to listen deeply to his clients in such a way that he blends their esthetic preferences with functional form and with economic perimeters. Throughout the years, Jesse has sustained and grown his practice despite several economic ups and downs. He did not expect to be an instant success, but was clear that he would create a competitive wedge in the marketplace by focusing on each residential customer to understand his or her unique needs.

A year ago, Jesse partnered with Karen, a designer who had just left a large industrial design firm in New York City. Karen was industrious and prided herself on her ability to sell products and consummate deals. Jesse wanted to expand his firm to establish a wider residential base and include the sale of products such as furniture and carpeting to existing and new customers. Karen seemed a perfect match.

Karen's expectation was to expand the business by 25 percent in the first year. She focused on defining and selling a few upscale product lines and establishing new accounts. Jesse noticed a concern; customers were sharing feedback about Karen. Karen wasn't listening. Too focused on her goal, she was selling by imposing her needs. When she was with the larger firm, her strategy seemed to work in the industrial market. Why wouldn't the same magic apply here? Jesse knew that the relationships he had established, and the potential for new ones, would be jeopardized if his partnership with Karen continued.

I asked Jesse, "What was your most significant lesson from your brief partnership with Karen?" He said, "It was not so much about Karen, but about me and my work style. To borrow your word, Cliff, my 'magic' is building relationships by listening to my customers. My design skills come second. If I work with someone else again, he or she will have to have the same value and expectation."

"Expectation?" I asked.

"Yes," Jesse replied. "To grow the business by attending fully to people's needs. You know, like suggesting a rubber floor for a laundry or picking a wall color by asking my client's daughter: 'What's your favorite color?' These details make the difference that people live with daily."

A New Direction

We are all headed in a new direction. If you can redirect yourself, the reward is mobility, adventure, and opportunity. Many of my clients know, conversely, that if they try to stay in one spot for too long, or if they hide, they will be devastated by the rapid changes or disappear in the quicksand of progress. Most important, they may miss out on fulfilling their own dreams.

Massive organizational, workplace, and marketplace change is an external call for you to follow your own dreams. Today's reality will force you to change, or it will pass you by. Joyce, a technical editor, called to schedule a consultation for herself and her husband. "The company I am working for has changed and the marketplace has done a number on my husband's business," she said. "Our careers seem to be going nowhere. I know what my dream is but have been unable to move it forward and my husband is frustrated running his business and isn't sure what his dream is. We are afraid and we need to take control of not only work, but of our lives."

Living your dreams is one of the best reasons for stretching and redefining the traditional notions of employment to embrace the notion of self-employment.

Living Your Dream: A Career that is True to Yourself

Joyce's priority was to spend more time with her children. Her professional goal was to find a position similar to the one she had but with one exception: The new position would be with an organization in which she could have a flexible work schedule. To her surprise, Joyce advanced on the traditional career ladder. Through a diligent networking effort, she found a position as technical editor and manager of custom publishing with a smaller publishing firm. Now, with a more flexible schedule, she is able to spend part of her time working from home. When she must attend meetings at the office, she can usually schedule them for when her children are in school. The price? She earns less money. But, she is living her dream.

Joyce's husband, Dean, the owner of a small insurance brokerage, took another path. He stepped off the traditional career ladder onto the career lattice. This meant facing the void of transition. "I see myself as someone with a huge amount of energy," he said. "For years I've been focused on building my practice and solving customer problems. What I've been doing is narrow; I don't feel creative. Besides, my market niche is being taken over by bigger companies. Even though I've made a good living, the business isn't meaningful enough to me to go up against the competition. I'd rather put my energy into figuring out what's next."

Initially, Dean asked, "Why am I so bored? Will finding something else take very long? How will I know when I've found something that is right for me?" These questions exemplify many such questions raised by people who are in career transition. They are healthy and necessary questions. Each represents a piece of a larger puzzle, a mini-goal. When the pieces of the puzzle are examined and all are put in place, achieving the dream is possible. During my sessions with clients, I assure them that with patience and persistence during this process we will answer their questions. Toward the end of a session, I give clients one of their questions back to them to answer. This gives them a goal during their transition. Dean asked, "Why am I so bored?" So I asked Dean to make a list of the things that are uninteresting to him at work and to share his list with me the next time we met.

After a three-month period of exploring his interests, accomplishments, values, and skills Dean closed his business and decided to pursue a sales or sales management position in the insurance industry. Soon Dean received four job offers. Dean, though gratified to receive the offers, turned them all down. "At this point," Dean commented, "I must be true to myself. The insurance business, working in a large company, is not me." This experience helped Dean to answer another one of his questions, "Is it running my own business that I've grown to dislike, or is it the insurance business?"

> *Adult worklife learning leads to*
> *understanding your own wisdom and*
> *the courage to live with and move*
> *beyond the doubts.*

Competing up the career ladder, stacking one professional job of a similar type onto another, wasn't the answer for Dean. When I asked him to list the things that he most liked doing, he said he enjoyed research, making things better, and solving problems. One of his skills was synthesizing information into a manageable system. Dean boiled down his passions into one phrase: "finding ways to do things differently." This phrase became a catalyst for Dean's progression.

With Dean's ingenuity, his knowledge of English literature, and his skill in research and problem solving, he secured a part-time job as an assistant librarian. This position might sound farfetched for an insurance broker, but he needed some income and a temporary work situation that felt good to him. This was an opportunity to use some of his skills; more important, with his wife's support and his own determination, he felt less pressure to retreat to the insurance business. Rather than push-ing for answers, Dean used the library job to notice what others did for a living and took time to assess what he wanted and needed.

Dean discovered that one way he could "do things differently" was to invent marketable goods. Months before instant coffee bags and bent-handled (back-saver) snow shovels came out on the market, Dean claims that he thought of these ideas. He had not pursued them because he didn't have any experience in transforming an idea into a reality. Dean's priority was to focus on what excited him. What he did with the idea was less important. The snow shovel was one idea. I proposed that he stay open to other means of "finding ways to do things differently." I said, "Think back to a time when you owned your own company, when you felt passionate, excited, and energized." Dean considered the question and then replied, "When I doubled my firm size from four to eight people and we climbed over the $5 million mark in sales." Then I asked, "What about this experience felt good to you?" "I was creative, a problem solver, and we were expanding. I was leading us forward, not only managing day-to-day operations."

Dean recalled a past experience when he had felt successful and fulfilled. Up to this point the experiences he recalled had coagulated into one seemingly cumbersome, uneventful whole wherein he was unable to delineate his strengths and weaknesses, his needs and passions. To embrace the self-employed attitude, we first must untangle and examine our past experiences, as Dean did. We then have a much sharper vision of the road behind us, which propels us forward along the road toward a more promising future.

We all have a rich warehouse of knowledge—
skills, values, interests, experiences—stored away but
accessible. For us to gain access to these hidden treasures,
we must deliberately take the time and effort to tell our stories,
untangle the past, notice what excites us, stay open to feedback,
evaluate who we are and what we really want, and take the risk of
transforming our thoughts and dreams into action.

To help Dean expand his vision further, I mentioned the market-place's need for people to create and develop micro-niche businesses. For example, a small boat builder that develops affordable, lightweight kayaks; a boutique consultancy that designs and disseminates cutting-edge software training; and a mini-technology company that produces specialized medical tools. Knowing about his proven ability and passion for finding ways to do things differently, I suggested that Dean look for businesses that were in the expansion stage and could benefit from his talents. Such companies would not be start-ups or established businesses. Rather, the best companies for Dean to investigate would be those that are looking for creative, flexible, and responsible people to help them harness and utilize their resources to develop new systems, products, and services; increase quality; and mentor others toward a common goal.

I suggested that he network with associates and colleagues, tap into the Internet, and read trade journals, newspapers, and magazines to locate these types of businesses. First, though, I recommended that Dean do an "I am looking for..." summary, an exercise that helps people refine their goals.

Dean's summary stated: "I am looking for a small service business that wants to expand. It has grown to a particular level, let's say to $2 million in sales, and it wants to grow to $10 million. I could help them because I am a creative individual who knows how to develop systems, lead people, and sell in a competitive marketplace."

Dean's summary raises an important question to ask his network: "Is there any company you know of that has these characteristics, or is there anyone you know of with whom I might talk who might have some suggestions?" As Dean received feedback from his network, he revised his summary to increase the probability of positive responses.

Take a moment and ask yourself, "What do I really like to do? What do I get excited about?" Try writing down your next step or goal—something that would bring you closer to doing what you really want to do. This exercise is relevant regardless of your work status—unchallenged, fired, laid off, never want to retire, or recent college graduate. The key is to sit with the question, not force an answer.

Depending on your particular situation, your goals can span a wide range of possibilities. You could be looking for a mentor, a raise, a promotion, ideas about what school would best suit your educational needs, clarification of your skills and values, a way to communicate more effectively with team members, or a partner to help you develop a business concept.

Dean is well on his way to adopting a self-employed attitude. At this time, he has not found a company match, but he feels supported and he is clear about his vision. As he expands his network, he will find a company in the expansion stage that matches his skills and passion. The marketplace depends on entrepreneurs hungry to lead niche businesses beyond survival to growth and expansion.

A Self-Employed Reality Check

At this point, you may be thinking, "I'm more self-employed than I thought. How can I improve my worklife?" You might also be wondering, "Just how self-employed am I?" Both questions are catalysts for continuing to learn about yourself and this concept. The self-employed inventory that follows will help you answer these questions. It is designed as a source of information and a guide for your learning.

Self-Employed Inventory

Think about these questions and how you typically behave on the job then answer "yes" or "no" to each. Write your answers to the questions on a separate piece of paper. If you answer "yes" to most of these questions, you can continue to fine-tune what you do and teach others. If you answered "no" to most of the questions, you have a sense of some of the ways that you think and act and of some of the things you need to learn.

1. Do you believe that your current job or customers are guaranteed?

2. Do you go beyond your job description?

   Do you volunteer for projects?

   Do you identify problems?

   Do you initiate solutions?

   Do you look beyond the hours you work to the task or job that needs to be accomplished?

3. Do you seek out others with whom to share ideas and advice?

4. Do you take an inventory of your skills and how they apply to others every four to six months?

5. Do you ask your customers—on a regular basis—what you can do to improve your service delivery or product quality?

6. Do you enjoy what you do at least two-thirds of the time?

7. Do you make a point to learn something new every week?

8. Do you ask questions rather than simply accept what comes your way?

9. Do you assess your options to change and risk to follow through with action?

10. Do you believe that you are responsible for your worklife?

Now look at your completed inventory. For question 2, you may have answered "yes" to identify problems but "no" to initiate solutions? In one area, identifying problems, you feel confident and have examples to prove your proficiency. On the other hand, initiating solutions is an area in which you've had little practice. Or perhaps you are used to thinking "that's someone else's job." In my work with hundreds of individuals inside and outside of organizations, I've heard how difficult it is to take initiative, and yet, how imperative it is to do so. In today's complex work environments, managers, owners, or colleagues can't possibly have all the answers. If initiating and presenting new ideas is one of your strengths, there are ample opportunities in the market-place for you. Try to remember this rule:

> *Initiate. For every problem you*
> *recognize, think of at least two*
> *solutions. Then, take the risk and*
> *present them.*

Customers will thank you for thinking things through and your boss will recognize you as an independent thinker who is able to make a contribution without being asked. It's as natural as sweeping your kitchen floor before your spouse asks you! As you read the following chapters, consider your answers to the self-employed inventory. Can you incorporate some of what you have learned as a means to turn a "no" into a "yes" or to improve your self-employed attitude?

Who's the Boss?
Check-In: Beginning the Process of Change with Yourself

Every question is an opportunity for understanding self, others,
and the world. It's not for judging, censoring, or faulting.

1. Sit back and remember what others said about you when you were a child. Was there a comment or compliment that you can remember that could be a clue to your uniqueness? Or is your memory a key to your magic?

2. Where do you go to reflect—examine who you are and what you may want to change in your worklife? When is the last time that you visited this place? Is it time for another visit?

3. What changes would you like to make in your worklife? What do you want more of? What do you want less of? Name one or two. Don't judge if you can make the changes or not, think of naming them as taking your first step forward.

4. Is there a question that you'd like to ask someone who might help you discover or clarify what you really want to do? Approach the person and ask!

5. Are you currently blaming someone for your lack of career mobility and/or job productivity? What power do you imagine they hold that you would like to have?

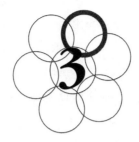

FACING THE DRAGON—
YOUR WORK FEARS

Replace fear with passion and purpose

EMPLOYED ATTITUDE
Dependent Mindset

If I just put my head down and work harder, I'll be safe. I can ignore my fears of knowing myself, losing my job, or understanding my passion and purpose.

SELF-EMPLOYED ATTITUDE
Independent and Interdependent Mindset

I will face the dragon—my worklife fears—and replace fear with passion and purpose. I will explore what I love, do more of what is in my heart, experience my joy, and productively contribute to others.

The dragon in all of us—individuals and organizations—is our fear of change. Fear of change holds back our potential, the contributions we could make, and our ability to experience the wonders and adventures of life. I can remember a time in my youth, for example, when I dreamed about living and working in California. I heard that San Francisco was a delightful city and that Big Sur was a spectacular place. But I was afraid to go. Disturbed and pained by my fear, I sought the counsel of George, a psychotherapist. After I talked for approximately 15 minutes, George looked straight at me and simply said, "Go." That is all I needed—validation for my passion, to express what was in my soul. His permission gave me permission to cut through my doubts. I connected with my hope for adventure and with my faith that in exploring new territory I'd be okay. Shortly after that session, I spent two of the best years of my life living and working in San Francisco. Fear could have held me back.

When we confront our fear, we can connect to hope
and learning. Then what we are afraid of can become
territory for exploration, opening fresh possibility.

Naming Fear

Traditional self-employment, owning one's own business, is an expression of self. Sometimes we can take this expression of self for granted or let our true feelings about it remain unexamined. Glenn, a colleague and business owner said, "When I tell some people I'm self-employed, I can see their eyes widen then shift as though wanting to escape the subject. I'm thinking we all need security, and I make my own…raising capital, answering to customers, examining my focus, and balancing the books. These responsibilities can be scary, but I figure there's a price that I pay to have control of my life. The alternative, working for someone else is even more frightening."

After years of persevering, conjuring up self-talk and learning from exploration, I have converted my need for security into creative energy and positively answered the question "Will I make the grade?" Today I'm comfortably resourceful but by no means complacently resolved. I'm entrenched in a worklife of traditional self-employment. Only now can I identify with Glenn and, too, can I more fully empathize with people who divert their eyes when the notion of self-employment is mentioned or who are set adrift in worklife transition.

I have earned my clients' faith, as they trust me with their fear and their hope, and I encourage them to let me know what they need from me. Shane, a vice president of development, was laid off from a start-up that lost its venture capital funding after a six-year struggle. She said, "As I proceed in my journey from discovering my strengths and what I want to do [I'm] confronting the big bad world. I'm guessing that I'll ask a hundred ridiculously simple questions. I'll need a lot of affirmation and, as necessary, gentle constructive feedback. I trust you with my fear, not to belittle it, dismiss it, or judge it in any way. Be particularly sensitive for awhile. My entire life I've struggled with these transitional times [that require] me to step outside the familiar. Once I get going, I'm usually okay, but getting started is excruciatingly painful."

When I first began my entrepreneurial journey, I recall Jamie, a friend, putting her head on my chest and saying, "Your breathing seems so shallow." At first, I was taken aback by her remark. I knew though, that her observation related to my fear—the unknowns—of starting a business. My body's rhythm was reflecting my anxiety.

But I learned Jamie's candor was a gift. Driving home from work, I'd put my hand on my heart to feel my breathing. Then I'd think about my breath and summon air, consciously, beyond my chest cavity into my abdominal area. I'd feel it and hold it there for a few moments.

With this practice, plus some satisfying successes—publishing articles and counseling clients—I began to relax more and feel better about myself and my choice to become an entrepreneur.

I'd like to think that those who are traditionally self-employed choose this path, at least in part, as an expression of their spirit—passion and purpose. In this book, although I'm not advocating that you own or start a business, I do support those of you who believe you can do work that resonates in your inner core. Your inner core is organic, a place with no preservatives, a central part of you. It is a place where safety and adventure coexist. Safety is the inner security that comes from knowing yourself; adventure, is the ability to risk or trade the known for the unknown. Safety and adventure coexist when you shed the artificial self—I should be _____ to know the natural self. I am _____ enough to step into, not to be coerced into, new frontiers. Over time, all the shoulds, oughts, demands, and distractions of life can diminish, but not extinguish, your passion and purpose. In all of us, there is the ability to breathe more deeply and live more authentically and closer to our passion and purpose.

Permission to Live Your Passion

I am passionate about the subject of why and how people become and contribute more of who they are in worklife. As I write this, I'm aware that I have a meeting to go to, but passion for expressing these thoughts seems to glue my bottom to my chair and keep my fingers pecking away on the keyboard. As well, I am drawn to people who are expressing their passion. Each face the unknown, daily as part of their fabric of self-expression, contribution, and making a living at what is most personally meaningful. Ben Rudnick, songwriter and musician, inspires me. Ben left the corporation and entire world of computer programming three years ago to pursue, music, his passion.

Since, Ben has produced two up-beat CDs for children and their families. His first *Emily's Songs*, is named after his daughter and has won the Parents Choice Award. In his second album, *Fun and Games*, "Jessica's Song," especially strikes me. It was written for a seven-year-old girl. Ben strums his guitar and sings, "Jessica, living free—be what you want to be."

When I observe Ben, I often think, "I admire Ben's spirit. It's like a bottomless tank of fuel." As it is so for Ben, passion or spirit is not in your head, it's in your heart, and it's bigger and more productive than left-brain stuff. For ignition, it needs your spark—attention and commitment.

Understanding that we are all self-employed gives you "permission" to do your work from your passion: to honor your spirit—your integrity. The reason to work through your fears and experience your passion is to do your best work and live a fuller life. Passion is your spirit. From here spring ideas and the energy to commit to meaningful promise and action. "I'm a soft-spoken leader," remarked one executive. "That's my power. Now that I know that, I want to find a place where I can use my being." This chapter will help you overcome your fears by demonstrating some specific ways that you can do your work and live your life practically, passionately, and purposefully.

We don't have to start with power, only with passion.
—Margaret J. Wheatley, *Turning to One Another*

I've survived and succeeded and I plan to continue to do so in our capitalistic economy. People I talk with casually, as well as my clients, plan to do the same. But like our forebears, who gave up the wilderness and the land, many of us have simply "joined up," clinging to the traditional models of work. As our organizational structures are being reshaped, we are being reshaped; our identities are being radically altered. Invisible T-shirts inscribed with company logos are sometimes impossible icons to take off. In many instances it takes skill, perseverance, patience, and time—a lot of it—to shed an organizational identity. Not to mention, courage. Organizations give us structure, compensation, a place to go, relationships with others, ego satisfaction and, for some, power. So why wouldn't it be painful, and seem nearly impossible at times, to shed an organizational identity? "For months after leaving my company," Francine said, "I felt like a brick strewn lot where an important building used to be." Dashel held his stomach as he said, "I know conceptually that I can no longer be loyal to my company in the same way, but I don't feel that way. I'll sue the company if they try to let me go." He was really saying, "I'm scared. I grew up in this company over the past 30 years. What would I do? Who would I be without it?"

Permission to Live Your Purpose

Purpose is what you are about. To know your purpose is to establish a taproot. This is a main root: stout, sturdy, and flexible. Your taproot enables you to "tap into" what nourishes you and keeps you growing. It will anchor and energize you in a blustery world. When the winds blow, you'll not only respond to what is urgent, but increasingly to what is important. Are you about...

1. Bringing joy to others?
2. Inspiring others to reach greater heights?
3. Seeing possibilities and seeking options?
4. Creating wealth?
5. Initiating social change to transform community?

6. Learning throughout life?

7. Visualizing and identifying what others rarely see?

8. Freeing others?

Notice that each purpose is broad and significant: a taproot. Your purpose naturally grows tributaries as you connect it with your passion, values, and dreams. And, it gives leeway for evolution and change over time as you experience, experiment, produce, and share with others.

If you don't become more conscious of your purpose, you or someone else will thwart your direction and dreams. As a healthy taproot gives rise to a tree with lush foliage, your true purpose gives rise to meaningful direction—jobs and projects. But here's the key to significant growth: to become more conscious of, and act on, your purpose. As you become more conscious of your purpose and act on it, you'll become more committed to it. You'll choose jobs and projects that honor what you're about, you'll struggle and champion to stay your course, and you'll better understand and build on your fertile past. You'll question more, feel unsettled when you're off purpose, honor you're uniqueness, and share your talents with others. You won't settle for boredom and you'll befriend ambiguity—tapping into your purpose, no matter how rocky the soil gets.

"I've been hiding," Megan commented, "distracted by too many interests and a lack of self-confidence. When I write about what I love to do, there are a wide variety of things. Recently I had a familiar experience where I found myself hidden, almost invisible. I vowed, 'I will shine now! I will not hide my light.' When I look back over the things I love, Cliff pointed out that there is a theme running through the stories—a purpose emerging—of bringing illumination to others. It's as though my Achilles heel of feeling hidden points to a great strength. Looking at what's most painful can often be a path that leads to purpose. I believe my purpose is 'shining in life'—both for myself and to provide a mirror for others to do the same. The questions I'm asking now are, 'How do I radiate more of who I am?' and 'How do I contribute my purpose to others?'"

Purpose Liberates

Purpose liberates the self and the other. For example, Doug, a financial planner, believes his purpose is peace of mind. Doug begins his conversation with prospective clients saying, "What I most care about is your peace of mind. My practice is focused on strategic and long-term planning, not quick fixes or bucks. I want to hear that you've slept well at night knowing that your investments are growing—not astronomically, but steadily." Up front, Doug's clarity of purpose qualifies his clients; as he articulates his purpose, while his clients have the opportunity to assess compatibility and determine if Doug's purpose is aligned with theirs. Simultaneously, Doug creates peace of mind for himself and his family as he builds a practice based on his belief. The chart below illustrates the purpose of others.

Purpose Liberates

Give Your Purpose to Others

Name	Profession	Purpose
Larry	Trust Attorney	Family Harmony
Charles	Sales Consultant	Making the Imaginable Possible
Lucy	Industrial Psychologist	Achieving Full Potential
Cliff	Worklife Counselor/Coach	Good Dream Reaching
Ned	Architect/Builder	Making the World a Better Place

To What Degree is *Your* Work an Expression of Your Purpose?

In asking this question I'm not hunting for or suggesting a utopian worklife. No job or career is flawless; the emphasis rather, is on degree. For example, I love my work but I can easily do without some of the administrative chores. I'm conscious of managing the transactional tasks, by degree, so that I spend more time on-purpose—writing, counseling, and thinking. I want to encourage you to reflect about and examine the core of your work—daily responsibilities and projects. To what degree are they compelling? Do you feel centered? Do you look up at the clock and wonder where the time went? Does what you are doing matter to you?

Your answers are meant for learning, not judgement. You can make choices, to be on-purpose, one more degree or two.

How Do You Keep Your Purpose Alive?

Do you dream precisely? Worry vaguely? Choose big enough? Learn a lot?

Jeff, a consultant and programmer, arrived at a fork in his career. Three quarters of the time he worked as a freelance programmer developing systems and software for corporate clients. During the remainder of the week, he dedicated himself to educating men and women about how to prevent violence at home and in the community. Although Jeff's formal schooling was in the area of electrical engineering, violence prevention and education had been a passion in his 20 years since college. As his reputation grew as a programmer and consultant, Jeff was asked if he would take on a fulltime position leading a group of programmers to consult with organizations. The new position would potentially increase his income several fold but would also stymie his passion.

Jeff said, "My parents instilled in me the importance of working for the 'good' of others. I've certainly served my corporate clients ethically and responsibly but when I reflect on my career path and experiences, I have a deeper calling. I've decided to commit myself more fully to my purpose: creating a safer world. I'm going to combine my consulting and leadership skills with my experience in violence prevention and education to start and fund an initiative that educates men and women about nonviolent measures and strategies. Although this full-time commitment is scary, it represents who I am."

Jeff remembered that his purpose was a taproot, burrowed deeply in his being. It defined his essence—what he's about. Whether or not your purpose is similar to Jeff's—improving relationships, building wealth, creating community, inventing new technology, or mediating for peace—you'll increase the likelihood of "keeping your purpose alive" if you practice the following:

Dream precisely. Set specific goals, think positively, and track results. Develop both small and large goals that align with your purpose. In addition, think positively—believe that every step you take is a chance to learn. Remember to adjust your goals as you gain experience but, whatever happens, don't give up your dream. To advance, ask your questions and learn from others, then tweak your actions accordingly. Don't take your actions for granted—write down your achievements to notice your gains. You'll count each gain as a step toward your dream.

Worry vaguely. Fear of the unknown is normal. But a conscious or unconscious emphasis on fear feeds worry and blocks out hope and possibly your dream. My clients in worklife transition have expressed worries such as: "People might laugh at me," "I might run out of money," and "Others can change, but I'm not so sure about myself." To them and to you I respond, "Let yourself worry 15 or 20 minutes a day, but during your other waking hours adopt a conscious hope strategy. Think and act one moment and/or one day at a time and cut yourself an "I'm human" break. Know that fulfilling your purpose will naturally elicit fears but that the other side of fear, if you choose it, is hope and gain.

Choose big enough. Hunt for a venue, project, or path that interests you deeply, connects with your purpose, and stretches you to fully use your strengths—your skills, values, beliefs, and aptitudes. If you don't choose a big enough challenge, you'll get bored and plateau prematurely. You'll ask, "Was all my experience and self-discovery for naught?" Conducting my We Are All Self-Employed seminar, for example, stretches me. It is vehicle to deepen and expand my purpose and passion and increase my productivity. I commit to a process of clarifying and transforming my ideas—as well as those of clients and colleagues—into focused, timely, and inspiring thoughts, stories, and exercises. You, my participants, keep me going with your learning and growth, your encouragement and comments.

Learn a lot. Give yourself permission to discover what you know and to uncover what you don't know. To write a 200 page book, I have written over a thousand pages. My words, sentences, and paragraphs are practice—my teachers—but only if I persist and give myself permission to learn to write better: more clearly, freely, precisely, and genuinely. Whatever your purpose, keep on learning. Ask many questions: explore how you do your work and how you might work more effectively and joyfully in your current or a new job. Review several ideas before you commit your time and energy to one. As you learn more, not only will you deepen and widen your worklife palette, but you will also win the prize: making choices that bring more of who you are to life.

Face to Face with the Dragon

Realize that you're not alone. Corporate Goliaths and smaller entities— small- to medium-size companies—are struggling to survive and compete. As many of you are learning and struggling not only to survive but also to go beyond survival, your expertise will be useful only for as long as you are benefiting an organization and its customers. I can remember a time not too long ago when a 43- year-old manager said, "If I could only get into a Fortune 500 company. I could stay there until my retirement." Organizations, whether they employ 100,000 or 10 workers, are not (and I doubt they ever were) safe harbors. They are, though, important places where people can make a contribution and earn a livelihood.

Challenge the dragon! To succeed, not simply to survive, we must change. The process is not necessarily easy, but we do it incrementally, practically, and creatively, and with a spirit for adventure. The alternative, living in fear, is decidedly no way to work or live.

Eliza is publications director at a small college in New England. She has extraordinary talent in her ability to attend to detail and see the big picture. She understands the needs of, and brings out the best in, others. She can organize, streamline, and utilize voluminous amounts of information and consistently meet deadlines. Her job brings her into a community that she deeply respects and supports, yet, for the past two years, Eliza has been challenged by pain in her hands and arms as caused by repetitive strain injury. For a writer, this is a major burden and source of anxiety. But, I believe that Eliza knows she is on her own path. Her congruence—matching who she is with what she does—helps her circumvent her discomfort and move toward her goals and those of the organization. Last year, she helped orchestrate the redesign and writing of the college magazine, Our College Today, which has received overwhelmingly enthusiastic feedback from the college's large constituency. To continue healing and stay on her own path, Eliza...

≡ Types in lowercase.

≡ Dictates her editorial comments on audio tape.

≣ Keeps reminding herself about what she enjoys. The other day she said, "I love interviewing people for feature stories. They trust me and tell me what's on their mind."

≣ Works in a fun and creative community where she feels a spiritual and intellectual connection.

≣ Uses voice recognition software provided by the college, which she can use at home and in the office.

≣ Offers new ideas as she dreams them up and sees the need.

≣ Thinks about how she can take on a challenge before she says "yes" or "no."

On the following page, I compare what it takes to live fearfully with what it takes to live passionately and purposefully. This comparison is important; you can make choices between the two. The list of values on page 87 shows what it takes to overcome any fears and how you can better express your passion and purpose. Among the points on this list, I'm partial to the phrase "courage to pursue what works for you." Helping individuals summon and use their courage to pursue what works for them is at the core of my counseling practice. If you do not learn this point, you will undoubtedly feel unhappy, uncommitted, depressed, or on edge. One of the worst feelings I've experienced is going through a prolonged period of being unhappy with my work. At such times, who I am is disconnected from my work; I watch the clock and ache inside. Unchallenged, I feel that my life is passing me by. Although I tell myself that being off my path is part of the process of finding my path, I can feel prey to these feelings and behaviors. I am dedicated to helping others work through, see the value in, overcome, and utilize similar experiences. Confronting yourself and giving birth to your joy do take courage. If you have read this far, though, courage and freedom are well within your grasp.

You Can Choose How You Live

Compare the two lists below. On a piece of paper, write down the items that describe you and your way of life.

To Live Fearfully	To Live Passionately and Purposefully
I react to and move from one thing to the next.	I defer gratification.
I stay closed to feedback.	I engage in continuous learning.
I do mostly what others say.	I pursue what works for me and consider others.
I discount what I am thinking and feeling.	I listen to my own internal messages.
I often retreat into a shell.	I am able to say, "This is who I am."
I resist support.	I can ask for support.
I rarely dream.	I can see all or part of my dream.
I give up too soon.	I respect tension and anxiety as part of the process of renewal and growth. Therefore, I persevere when things seem out of control or least hopeful.

What It Takes to Express Your Passion and Purpose

Patience, to defer gratification

Self-Permission, to engage in continuous learning

Courage, to explore and pursue what works for you

Openness, to hear feedback from others and to listen to your own internal messages

Boldness, to say, "This is who I am!"

Humility, to ask for support

Vision, to see all or part of your dream

Tenacity, to persevere when things seem out of control or least hopeful

Choose Courage and Recognize Your Freedom

On October 31, 1998, at the Caribbean Conference on Human Resource Development, I presented the concepts of *We Are All Self Employed* to a Haitian private and public sector group in Port au Prince. Marlene Gay, executive director, prefaced the conference with these remarks: "What other place [than Haiti] would be better fit for this plea for a complete paradigm switch than the capital of a nation whose people experience the switch from the paradigm of slavery to that of liberty and independence."

At the end of my presentation, the audience applauded exuberantly. I imagined they were applauding for the hard-won freedom and hope they felt in the moment, and the desire to express more of it. One gentleman stood up and commented, "We all want more freedom, but how do we express ourselves—become more entrepreneurial—in a society that keeps us back? In the United States you are free. If you have an idea you can give it life. You can turn your dreams into business."

I thought to myself that too many of us here in the United States take our freedom of expression for granted. We can do what we want—follow our hearts' desires if we persevere and consciously recognize the unique democratic infrastructure that supports each one of us. When I have fear about expressing myself, I often think about my trip to Haiti and remember this gentleman's words.

Suspending Fear: Passion in Process

Walter, a marketing manager with a communications company, was dreading a performance appraisal meeting with his boss. The organization had been downsizing for the past two years; colleagues in his division and in others had been laid off. Several projects he had been working on for the past six months had not succeeded, which added to his anxiety. Unlike in the past, there were more fits and starts and fewer results to report. Walter, speculating that he would hear bad news at the meeting, sought my services to discuss his anxiety and to explore ways of supporting himself and the company.

Walter was clearly waiting for the boom to drop so I asked him if he would try suspending his speculations. He agreed. "If you didn't have fear," I asked him, "what would you do in this situation?" After some thoughtful moments, he answered, "I'd not only listen to what my boss had to say, but I would tell my boss what was on my mind. I'd tell him about the changes that I saw in my job and in the organization."

Like many of us, Walter had learned *not* to question his boss. "Don't question, but do ask." This message has been drilled in and is deeply embedded in our psyches. Our parents, teachers, coaches, and managers—all bosses—say in one way or another "I'm in control," "I know better," or simply "Do what you're told—because I said so." These messages teach us to second-guess ourselves. They inhibit our creativity, spontaneity, our spirit for adventure. We learn to follow rather than to participate, invent, and contribute. Societal conditioning facilitates forgetting. I'm here to remind you that you're the boss, too.

It seems that rapidly and painfully, the tides are shifting. Companies are learning that they *need* people who question and contribute—those who understand their own needs and business's goals, see what needs to be done today and in the long term, and are prepared to participate in change. As their structures flatten, companies are collaborating more with workers. Problem solving increasingly requires specific expertise, as intensified competition calls for effective and efficient team participation. Workers like Walter are getting the message that it is their responsibility to take an active role in their own development as well as that of the company.

Walter took control by stepping back to analyze what he had been doing and under certain conditions. After reviewing his project requirements he realized that his job primarily involved researching and planning project feasibility, not managing people, in a work environment that was trying to stabilize. He saw that he was no longer acting as a marketing manager, a role perhaps better suited to a growing environment. Clarifying his current role and seeing it within the context of a changed corporate environment became a crucial catalyst for establishing what he called a "conversational approach," as opposed to a subordinate one, for the meeting he feared.

As Walter talked about what he actually *did*, he learned what his job really entailed. Many of my clients don't know what they do, they just "do." To represent themselves or navigate unfamiliar territory, they must find the words that describe what they do and create a bridge toward choice and positive change. With this insight, Walter brought his own agenda to the meeting. He asked questions, made comments, and shared solutions—but he did not try to control his boss's behavior or predict what the outcomes might be. One of the things we can ask ourselves in our workplaces is...*If I didn't have "fear" what would I do within my job or career?*

Find a quiet spot, and for a couple of minutes give this question some thought. To calm you and facilitate your thought process, sit comfortably and think about your breath. Take in air, letting it travel to your abdominal area, and hold it for a few moments. Expel the air slowly. Again, hold your breath for a second or two. Repeat this several times and keep your eyes closed as you do. Now you can return to your normal breathing pattern. Write down on a piece of paper the first thing that comes to your mind. Writing down your fear is a way to get it out of you and face it. Acknowledging your fear is the first step to moving beyond it. Now, write down one action step that you might take to overcome your fear and go; try it out.

Fear constricts and binds you; it keeps you from risking new ways of solving your problems and so gives rise to still more self-defeating behavior. Fear, incidentally, is always fear of some future thing. I have observed that as soon as a person confronts or challenges whatever he is afraid of, the fear vanishes.

—*Virginia Satir, Peoplemaking*

One of Walter's fears was that his boss would not listen to him if he shared what was on his mind. An action step he took was to prioritize and write out his agenda so that he could present his thoughts succinctly.

Walter's Agenda:

1. *Talk about what he had accomplished within the context of a changed organization.*

   Walter's recent accomplishments, although different from those in the past, were aligned with present organizational needs. Through his foresight, his flexibility, and his ability to analyze the current situation, he had created a different yet necessary role.

2. *Share what he and others were feeling about the organization.*

   Walter had noticed the dissatisfaction and struggles of his colleagues. They, as he, were reluctant to talk about this despair. Rather than letting fear dominate, Walter shared some of his feelings and those of his coworkers. His boss listened, for he too had feelings about the changes in the company.

3. *Ask specifically what the current goals of the division and the organization were.*

   Walter began to see that it was his responsibility to seek out information. With this information he could make choices and influence others. Without it, he had much less control.

4. *Continue making a contribution.*

   Using the information he received from his boss, Walter could make specific suggestions about how he could continue to contribute.

His boss listened. Walter's performance appraisal meeting turned into a constructive conversation and a gateway for future collaboration with his boss. Walter is still working as a marketing manager with the same communications company, but he is not the same person. Walter has learned that by confronting his fear, changing the way he thinks about a situation, and taking action, he can make a difference in his own life and make a contribution to the organization.

Below you'll see the benefits of expressing your passion and purpose. One benefit is that you'll feel a greater inner sense of security and express it outwardly. This aspect is a joy. Believe it or not, you can earn less money and feel more secure! The security comes from feeling that you are doing work that is part of, not apart from, you. No one can take that from you. It's yours.

Benefits of Expressing Your Passion and Purpose

You will...

≡ feel better—more energetic, more whole.

≡ attract people with similar values.

≡ experience a GOOD tired feeling at the end of the day.

≡ find a job or project that fits with your goals and skills.

≡ feel a greater inner sense of security and express it outwardly.

≡ make a unique contribution to the world.

All self-actualized people have a cause they believe in, a vocation they are devoted to. [They] seem to do what they do for the sake of ultimate, final values, which is for the sake of principles which *seem intrinsically* worthwhile. They protect and love these values, and if the values are threatened, they will be aroused to indignation, action, and often self-sacrifice.

—A. H. Maslow, *The Farther Reaches of Human Nature*

An Agenda for Unchallenged Workers

Unchallenged workers can borrow from Walter's agenda to create opportunity for themselves and their organization. If you are unchallenged, your agenda might look like this:

Agenda for Developing a "Self-Employed" Attitude

1. *Inventory your skills and accomplishments at least every six months.*

   Write down specific examples that illustrate your skills and accomplishments.

2. *Seek out information about company/division goals.*

   Network with colleagues and workers in other divisions. Find out if new products and services are being planned. There may be an opportunity for you.

3. *Discover ways to make a contribution.*

   Match your skills and accomplishments with company/ division goals.

4. *Share your plans and feelings with your colleagues and manager.*

   Find support for and get feedback on your ideas. Ask others for their help to clarify and align your desires with company/division goals.

Your Present Situation

Don Quixote, Cervantes's courageous hero, charged the windmills, which were symbols of change. His advances were thwarted by progress, the windmill's arms. The windmills of today—rapidly advancing technology, worldwide unrest, and ceaseless global competition—are impossible to defy. Despite gallant efforts—individual or organizational—fighting to maintain the old ways or holding on to the status quo, you will eventually be blown over by the windmill's powerful force.

The reality of we are all self-employed calls for self-leadership—taking responsibility for job productivity and career mobility and for contributing to others. Thinking, "My job is safe; I doubt I would ever lose it" is an unrealistic belief. You can work very hard, as thousands of workers have experienced, and still lose your job.

Quixotic heroics may very well feed your fantasies, but to challenge the dragon within and outside yourself, you must first understand your present work situation. The following exercise will help you to challenge the dragon—confront your fears regarding change—by exploring how you and your job have changed. This is a bold step toward seeing your abilities and making other changes.

The purpose of the exercise to help you see your current work situation: how it has changed and how you have changed. Seeing your current actions listed in the "Now" column and comparing them with your former activities listed in the "Then" column will help you assess your progress and make future plans. You may learn, for example, that you have made more changes than you thought. On reflection, you may feel especially good about your present ability to collaborate with a team. Once you are more conscious of this change, ask yourself, "What skills have I developed? Which do I want to develop further?" Is one of your skills your ability to negotiate with other team members?

You and Your Job: Then and Now

More than likely, over the past six months or even less you and your job have changed. Here are two examples: 1) You used to take orders from your boss but now you contribute ideas to a team that includes your boss, and 2) You were managing people, whereas now you are managing projects. Other examples are shown in the chart below.

Then	*Now*
I basically did what my boss asked.	I collaborate more with a team.
I managed 20 people.	I manage projects, not people.
I worked at the company office.	I work part-time from home.
My accounts were scattered through a region.	I'm now focused on a one major city market.
Professional education was not a priority.	I'm constantly reading professional journals and books.

On a piece of paper, draw a similar chart. Label one column "Then" and the other "Now." Think of ways in which you and your job have changed. Be specific. In the "Then" column, write down one of the characteristics of your past. Opposite each "Then" response, in the "Now" column, give an example of the way you or your job situation is now.

When the Organization Changes

The organization, too, is faced with the powerful arms of change. Over the past few decades I've heard about, and met, too many executives who have chosen their million-dollar bonus at the cost of X number of lay-offs. They have forgotten to ask themselves, "How much compensation is enough?" or, "How many people must be laid off to pay my salary?" My hunch is that fear and greed drive their actions. They don't think about, or at least not for too long, the inequity and the havoc they create in others' lives.

I can hope that with time, personal experience of job loss, and media exposure, those who wield the axe might change. But, I'm not banking on it. I've counseled people who have been laid off as many as five times in the past seven years and it's not until he or she takes charge, and changes, that their lives improve. Samara said, "The company was making plenty of money, but this year they weren't as profitable as last. My boss announced to our technology group that all 10 of us would lose our jobs. Some were demoralized, others were angry, and I was worried at first but then energized. With a severance package in hand, I plan to examine my needs and take control of my career."

Cameron said, "I spent from my mid-30s to my early-40s reporting to the president's of four mid-sized companies. I'd open up and expand sales territories by growing the sales force. And, inevitably when there was a change in leadership, they'd get rid of me too. I'd feel deflated, but after a few weeks, I'd pump myself up to hunt for a similar job." I said, "I'll bet that pattern got old." "It did," Cameron responded. "Finally, I decided the boards that ran those companies weren't about to change to suit me. I took some time off…went to Alaska to cool off! Since, I've started a business consulting with organizations to help them increase their sales. Now, when the job is done, I leave."

To break the cycle of fear—others controlling your worklife—you, not they, must change from an "employed" to a "self-employed" attitude. Repeating the same behavior, no matter how determined you are, is not good enough.

Since the original publication of this book in 1994,
organizational change has not slowed down. Change
has increased, and will continue to do so. This is all the
more reason for you to take charge of your worklife.

Replace Fear with Passion

Joanne, a planning manager with a *Fortune 50* company, felt confined in her job. She had a prestigious title, was earning plenty of money, her boss considered her a valued expert, and she had earned the respect of her colleagues as the first woman in the company to attain such a position. Although she appeared successful to others, Joanne had grown tired of planning and wanted to move into a leadership role where she could use her creative talents. Still, she felt conflicted because she was afraid to give up her status and income. She liked her colleagues and believed the company she had been with for the past five years was on the verge of becoming a recognized leader in the industry. Joanne asked, "How can I move on in my career to where I feel passionate about my work, remain visible, and also earn a good living?" Joanne's intent was not to leave but to help lead the company through an organizational restructuring process. To "let go," she found it helpful to see herself as self-employed—to see that only she could be responsible for her career mobility. Even though her boss recognized her as a valued candidate, from his point of view she was a valued expert in the "right" position.

Joanne needed to challenge the dragon. She was a superb problem solver and initiator of solutions, but rather than continuing to plan and do, she needed to step back and take an inventory of her skills, values, and interests and to assess how she might apply these in the company. As a result, she identified two skills for which she felt passionate and wanted to market: leading and communicating. Leading involved seeing and articulating how the culture needed to change and communicating included her ability to influence, negotiate, and build a team around a common goal. Her inventory gave her plenty of marketing material, but she still needed to confront her fears. She isolated two: 1) reprisal from her boss if she moved and 2) her own reservations about her ability to take on a leadership role.

Joanne talked about her fears as a means of airing and resolving her feelings. Regardless of your level, compensation, or professional expertise, it is crucial to your mobility to talk about your feelings. Often this process is overlooked or consciously denigrated as the "soft stuff." What looks "soft," however, may be the hardest obstacle to overcome. Joanne went on to formulate a plan for building a bridge between her current situation and her future goals. At a company meeting, she caught wind of an opportunity whereby she could potentially help Laurel, a vice president, streamline her division. Joanne met with Laurel to share her knowledge about some of the problems Laurel was facing and to propose how she herself, in a leadership role, could help the vice president plan, communicate, and implement change. Joanne then accepted Laurel's offer to take on a part time leadership role.

The other part of Joanne's plan was to view the shift toward leadership as one-half of her job. She remained active as planning manager, at least for a while, as she tested her new role. She is now making program contributions to another division, programs that could be adopted as models for change for the entire company. She is gaining marketable experience, developing visibility in another part of the company, and feeling more passionate about her work. She has a parachute or fallback position—a continuing relationship with her former boss and colleagues should things not work out as expected. And, she realizes that not even this parachute comes with a guarantee. Joanne discovered that letting go of her past and moving toward her passion took courage and ingenuity. None of us can or should make a career move by taking one quantum leap. Developing a "self-employed" attitude—overcoming your fears and living your passion—is an incremental process.

There is a Price for Ignoring Your Passion

The price for remaining stuck in an unrewarding job is a gnawing, tired, angry feeling of unfulfillment, a sense that you could be *doing* more with your life and that you could be *feeling* better about what you do and how you contribute to others. Doing what you really want to do, even partially, isn't easy. I've witnessed numerous individuals who give up at the halfway point or do not try at all. They choose to hear, "Getting a job is tough," "Finding another position in the company is nearly impossible," or "Why speak your mind? The company doesn't care." People buy into the majority or a belittling voice before exploring alternatives. They bury their passion under yet another layer of fear or skepticism and do only what is practical: charging obediently and blindly, against that fire-breathing dragon.

Don Juan teaches Carlos Castaneda about the notion that "we are all self-employed" in *The Fire from Within*:

> To have a path of knowledge, a path with a heart, makes for a joyful journey...and is the only conceivable way to live. We must then think carefully about our paths before we set out on them, for by the time a person discovers that his path "has no heart," the path is ready to kill him [or her]. At that point few of us have the courage to abandon the path, lethal as it may be, because we have invested so much in it, and to choose a new path seems so dangerous, even irresponsible. And so we continue dutifully, if joylessly, along.

Lunch with a Colleague

From my perspective, writing a book is a collaborative journey. My colleagues and friends give support and contribute ideas, and I gather and synthesize information and put the words on paper. Over the years I have made an effort to invite people who have been helpful to join me for a thank you breakfast or lunch. Inevitably, our conversations focus partially on our careers.

I hadn't seen Luca, an art director, in almost a year, although we'd had several telephone conversations. While I was writing this book, Luca reviewed a draft of the manuscript and made several useful and heartfelt comments. When we sat down to lunch, I was startled by Luca's lack of eye contact. For the first 10 minutes of our meeting he sat hunched over, looking down at his plate and asking me questions about my life. I was puzzled and asked, "So what's going on for you?" Luca's eyes met mine. He paused, then said, "I'm feeling confused, lost. I'm stuck in the same place, working part time. I don't seem to be getting anywhere with my career."

Luca is a 55-year-old man who grew up in a small town, became successful in advertising and public relations, got knocked off the ladder, and is now on his own—self-employed. Luca has pride and, like many people I've met, is afraid of stumbling and bumbling in the marketplace. "I've paid my dues," Luca reminded me—a common proclamation. "I wish I had learned at 23 what Paola, my daughter, already knows about herself and her career." "What does Paola know?" I asked. Luca began a verbal list, "She takes risks, trusts her intuition, believes [that] change is good and it's OK to make mistakes. She champions herself and doesn't wait for others' opinions before she takes action."

I thought that was quite a list and said, "I know what you mean. I wish I'd known those things when I was 23!" Luca said, "Another thing,

I doubt she has this list written down anywhere and I'm not sure how conscious she is of her attributes. She doesn't have a mentor; she just lives in these ways. Sometimes it's hard to believe we both live in the same world. Paola isn't afraid to make things happen."

As Luca talked, I looked at him and thought to myself that Paola did have a mentor, and that if more people became conscious of and wrote down constructive behaviors for overcoming their fears, they would learn to trust their intuition. Their list would become part of their plan for acting on their intuition. "Luca," I said, "Paola's words are a template for change. They give her inspiration and courage." "Her words are a golden template," Luca added. "I need to learn from her. It's time I stop hiding behind my plans and start meeting more people. I need to tell them what I can do for them." "Luca, I want to remind you," I said. "Paola has had a mentor...you." Luca's eyes widened and he smiled. Before we parted Luca wrote down his "golden template" and handed it to me.

Luca's Golden Template:

I will . . .

- ≣ talk about my feelings.
- ≣ risk sharing my ideas with others.
- ≣ plan, then test my plan. I won't just plan, plan, plan.
- ≣ meet with friends more often for support.
- ≣ champion myself, as Paola does. I won't use the excuse to rely on the opinions of others before I take action.
- ≣ view mistakes as stepping stones.

You may want to create your own golden template. Think of two or three guiding principles—messages that you could consistently give yourself to grow and progress in your work and your life.

Patience is an Active Process

We have explored the fear of change and addressed the importance of knowing the current realities of the workplace. Before we go further, I want to address impatience as an obstacle to your passion, purpose, job productivity, and career mobility. Unfortunately, in our society—in organizations, schools, and families—we get little support for the rediscovery process. Messages like "Getting there shouldn't be such a struggle" abound and feed our impatience. The resulting "shoulds" and expectations to achieve more quickly than the reality allows block our rediscovery—passion, mobility, and productivity. Statements like, "I'm too old for this; I should know where I'm going by now" or "This shouldn't take so long" or "I should do what others think is best" inhibit our progress. They bury our inner voice and inhibit the discovery of our true needs and wants.

Believing we are all self-employed requires that we make an active cognitive shift from "I should" to "I need" or "I want." The needs or wants are available to us when we pause and learn to be patient, primarily with ourselves. "I'm 43 years old and I'm burning out," complained Ron, a successful entrepreneur. "I've developed this pattern of going from one thing to the next. My career is important to me, but I can't go on this way." Ron believed that he should always be doing things. Exhausted by this pattern, he no longer enjoyed running his business. After we talked at length about the pattern, I asked Ron if he could learn to be patient with himself as he tried some new ways of coping with change and reestablishing his career. I said, "Ron, I think that patience—calming yourself—is different than waiting—or finger tapping—for something to happen. If you can learn to question and be open to unexpected answers, observe and not judge, and enjoy the moment more, you'll feel more relaxed, make better decisions, and eventually find your next opportunity." Ron seemed relieved. He needed permission from someone else to readjust his pace and take a look at what was no longer working in his life.

Over several months, Ron discovered that being patient was an active learning process that involved making daily decisions. It was important for him not to charge into another business or a box that would put him back into his familiar yet debilitating frenetic pace. Rather, with patience, Ron learned to name his feelings, talk about the skills and values most important to him, and experiment with how he might get his needs and wants met by working part time. I often say to my clients, "Slow it up." Many are relieved to receive permission to try another way.

Patience Can Lead to Passion

The following list suggests some ways that you can be patient as a means toward living your passion.

What to Do:

- ≣ Share your ideas, but hold off and think carefully before committing to action.
- ≣ Explore, be curious and gather information.
- ≣ Share your honest, intuitive opinion.
- ≣ Do things step by step and follow through.
- ≣ Confront problems and trust that you'll find solutions.
- ≣ Tell others that you haven't made a decision yet, but you will get back to them.

≣ Do part time work as you search for what you really want.

≣ Work for the common good.

Working for the common good—that is, finding your path and the work you want to do—means you'll inevitably work for the good of others. Ruth, a public relations specialist, has found an expression for her passion: influencing others. She is dedicated to serving her clients in the software industry, helping them deliver unique messages through the media and run profitable businesses. She is giving them her communications expertise and her passion. They, in turn, are providing tools for customers to do their work more effectively.

Stepping Beyond Fear: Caring and Respecting

"In meetings," began Martha, an administrator, "I'm usually the one who makes sense of and exposes what the real issues are. It's as though I'm a voice for others." In a consultation with Martha, I asked, "How do you know that you are expressing what others are thinking?" "People sit up and their eyes open wide," she replied. "Often, after a meeting, there are those who say, 'You spoke for many of us.'" As she told her story, Martha glowed but then quickly dismissed her talent as nothing special. I've spoken with several professionals like Martha who make statements and tell stories about their talents. They say, "I can see the bigger picture and describe what I see to others," or "As a manager, I bring out people's best talents, and as a result they feel good about their work and become more productive," or "I enjoy and am challenged by shifting into different roles." They proceed to back up their statements with stories. But, just as Martha did, they pass off their talent by saying, "Big deal."

In these situations I am quick to say, "Take care of and respect what seems to be natural to you. Passion comes in many forms, some not as obvious as others. You can take care of and respect your abilities by suspending your judgment and practicing curiosity and observation. Notice other people's eyes and posture, and become aware of what they say. They are telling you about you."

Another way to respect and care for your talent is to keep a journal. Write down specifically what you did and how you felt in the process. On a sales call, for example, do you "listen" to your client? Do clients then consistently respond by buying your product or service, or do they refer others to you? If you have already written about this scenario several times in your journal, most likely you have a talent or a skill that you've honed: listening. Don't ignore your talent, even though it may seem obvious to you; take care of and respect it. Document your specific behavior and note how you use your listening skills. Do you paraphrase what your clients say? Do you share some of your own experiences that might mirror your clients'? Is your eye contact direct and sincere? These are the skills that have made you a successful salesperson. Take care of and respect them as you call on clients. Share them as you step toward a "self-employed" attitude and look toward enhancing your career.

Who's the Boss?

Check-In: Facing the Dragon—Your Work Fears

*Every question is an opportunity for understanding self, others,
and the world. It's not for judging, censoring, or faulting.*

1. When you hear of or think about the term "self-employment,"
   what feelings and images emerge?

2. Can you name a time in your worklife when you confronted
   your fear? What did you do? What happened as a result?

3. Take a walk or find a comfortable place to sit. Now think back
   to your childhood and what you loved to do. Think about
   settings: the beach, a neighbor's yard, the park, the
   neighborhood sandbox, a snowfield, or your room. Did you like
   to watch people? Did you like to build things? Did you play
   sports? Did you imagine things and tell scary stories? Search for
   passion and purpose embedded in your answers.

4. How do you keep your purpose alive? Do you set specific
   goals? Do you think about how you spend the majority of your
   time and if the tasks at hand truly suit you? Do you ask
   questions or let fear stifle your curiosity?

5. Who do you trust to support you as you make changes in your
   worklife? Is there someone in your past who you have not
   talked with in awhile? Is there a new person in your life with
   whom you might share your thoughts and concerns?

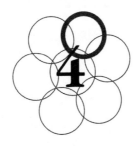

INTEGRATING

INDEPENDENCE AND

INTERDEPENDENCE

Be yourself and collaborate with, and contribute to, others

EMPLOYED ATTITUDE
Dependent Mindset

I am dependent on the company and customers. They know what I do best and what is best for me. They will know what I want and take care of me.

SELF-EMPLOYED ATTITUDE
Independent and Interdependent Mindset

I will integrate independence—knowing and being myself—and interdependence—collaborating with and contributing to others.

Transition from summer to fall is ushered in by warm days and cool nights, turning leaves, and crisp apples. Every autumn I pay special attention to another sign of seasonal change: the flocks of wild geese migrating south, whose majesty inspires a sense of wonder and joy. They also symbolize to me the bridge between independence and interdependence, the subject of this chapter.

Every one of these birds is *independent*, distinctly airborne and propelled by its own power. Each is also interdependent, taking cues from one another and flying in exquisite formation. They seem free yet purposeful. They are organized yet unrestricted as they fly toward a common goal.

The geese fly for days tirelessly, rotating positions, each taking a turn at the helm. They share the leadership responsibility so that burnout is rare and if one does falter two others move forward to support the one in trouble. Imagine if individuals and organizations learned to function this way!

Dependent on the System

This chapter is for those of you who feel shackled by the constraints of dependence on an organization and are looking for the support to be yourself, do your best work, *and* collaborate with and contribute *to* others. Many of the individuals I counsel and coach appear successful from an outsider's point of view. They have things, titles, and power. But, paradoxically, they are dependent, driven by, and beholden to a system. The system is composed of their clients, customers, parents, family, spouse, organization, *and* themselves. "My problem," said Robert, a chief investment officer, "is that I'm about to become a partner in the firm but I'm not sure I want the position. Fifteen years ago I sort of fell into what I'm doing...I've been successful, although my success has not really been by design." And Audrey, a dentist said, "I had no interest in dentistry but I decided to apply to dental school because a friend was doing it, and I felt that I was smart and was expected to do something with my life. I had no idea what was involved in being a dentist. My only exposure was being a dental patient. I talked to no one about the work, not my parents or school advisor, not even my friend in whose footsteps I was following. After over a decade as a practicing dentist, I see that many things about being a dentist involve aptitudes that I lack—fine motor skills, sustaining relationships, and quick decision making. To this day I ask myself why I didn't play to my strengths? Instead, I've been prey to my weaknesses. Why didn't I talk with others and explore more apt possibilities?" We are all part of the system in varying degrees. This is not a judgment but rather a practical observation designed to free and inspire you. Many of you may wonder, "Have my choices been of my design?" Others may ask, "What is in my control and how do I go about taking control?"

Together we are all going through life alone.

—Lily Tomlin

Dependence is Not Support

Dependence is *not* support. Support is the direction that mentors give their protégés. It is also part of the synergy athletes must have to form an exceptional team or that world leaders must utilize to create peace. Without support, individuals and teams could not function effectively and our world would likely be uninhabitable. Support is a vital form of sustenance and can be the underpinning for growth and change. Several years ago, after 19 years of marriage, my friend Greg went through a divorce. For about six months, we had coffee together once a week. I never said much about his situation, but he knew I cared. To this day, Greg reminds me that sitting with him or, in his words "just being there," pulled him through a devastating time.

I often receive telephone calls from people I have never met who want to explore the potential match between my counseling service and their goals and personality. To begin our conversation, I ask the individual to share a bit about their current worklife situation. From the start, the best support I can offer is to listen. "I worked for 12 years at a health care facility," Lila said, "and was laid off. Without thinking too much about what I really wanted to do, I started looking for another job right away. It took me eight months to find the part time project management position I have right now. Last week I was told that this job would end in a few months. My history is to dive right into another job search. I don't want to do this again. But in truth, I don't really know what I'm interested in pursuing. I couldn't tell you what interests me. I've not slowed down to think about my needs. I've been too busy with two young children. Fortunately, I have a supportive husband, but he has his limits as to how much he can listen to about my work concerns. We seem to go round and round the same issues…it's been years in this pattern! I think I'm at the point of needing outside help. Am I odd? Are there others you've talked with in this fix?"

"Lila," I said, "I've talked with many people in your situation. Like you, they have admirably put their heads down to do whatever they've needed to do to survive. Cumulative unhappiness and external circumstances, in your case job loss, raises questions such as, 'What do I really want in my life? and What truly interests me?' Besides, you're at midlife, a natural time for you to explore and create what you want in the second half of your life."

"I have to face my unhappiness," Lila said. "I've been muddled for years. Just saying the things I've said to you helps me to feel better. Curiously, I feel less muddled."

Support in its most positive light gives people hope and teaches them to be their best authentic selves in their work. There is something pure about support. Dependence, on the other hand, teaches people to suppress who they are—to sublimate their passion, resist their creativity, and compromise their values. As the job market fluctuates and corporations restructure, many professionals today feel more dependent as a result. People believe it when they hear, "You'd be lucky to find another job." Or, they capitulate and think, "Why should I even ask or look? There just aren't any jobs." Or, they adopt—consciously or unconsciously—a dispassionate attitude, "I have no power. I'll keep my head down and hope for the best."

Dependence is also rooted in another extreme—what Sarah, a systems manager, referred to as the "golden handcuffs." She said, "That's when the company paid me so much that I couldn't afford to leave. Out of one side of my boss's mouth he told me I was doing a good job and reminded me that I was earning in the six figures. But I was not allowed to attend the organization's strategy meetings. It was killing me to compromise my values. I didn't have decision-making power. Finally, to the disbelief of my boss, my colleagues, my parents, and my friends, I left."

I clung to my business mother for 26 years. I valued myself because of who IBM thought I was.

—Albert, a former project team leader at IBM

Dependence is as Impure as Support Can be Pure

Dependence is our responsibility. Those who accept it and choose to remain dependent live by the creed, "As long as they pay me and I get my benefits, I'll do what they want." Some people live by another creed, equally grounded in dependence. "I'll manipulate the system (or at least try to) to get what I want." Christyn, a corporate systems executive, was on maternity leave. Her yearly compensation package included a substantial bonus based on individual and organizational performance criteria. After three months at home with her newborn, Christyn decided not to return to work. It was September and she expected her bonus the following January. Christyn called her boss and asked, "If I decide not to come back to work, could you still pay me my annual bonus?" Her boss said, "Over my dead body! If you want to return to work for the rest of the year, *then* you might be eligible for your full bonus." Traditionally "self-employed" people get paid for what they do—their performance. This is how they earn their living. Christyn found out we are all self-employed. Her dependent, manipulative request went unrewarded.

Dependence is...

- ≣ feeling constrained, as though you are living someone else's life.

- ≣ working in a profession that someone else chose for you; fear and obligation are the reasons you continue.

- ≣ staying closed to feedback about yourself and changes in the world.

Independence

Independence—or your freedom—is a lifelong, evolutionary and at times revolutionary process that requires courage, patience, awareness, wisdom, and the ability to compete. In the United States and other parts of the world we have "constitutional" independence, a legal right. But "live" independence—actively pursuing your dreams and serving others—is a different story. One does not automatically guarantee the other. My grandfather came here from Dier El Gazelle, Lebanon because he heard America was a free land. He lived his freedom—persevering, innovating, and producing—independent of contradictory opinions. While many of his peers had positions, or climbed the ladder, he didn't have words for the way he worked. He made choices like letting his tenants forgo payment of their rents during the great depression: he burned the grass.

Our ancestors earned their independence, but their legacy has been lost over the years. Sometimes our independence seems elusive as we battle the dragon, our thoughtless activity, and our unexamined priorities. We believe that independence is reserved for the elite. We seek and wait for approval before we make a suggestion or decision, invent something new, or follow our dreams. During a 12-year period, Sam, an office equipment salesman, fell unwittingly into a web of dependence that included repeat clients, financial rewards, and career advancement. To an outsider, Sam's situation might have looked pretty good, and for a time it was. With another promotion in the offing, he questioned, "Is this my destiny? My colleagues think this offer is a great opportunity, but I feel I need a change." As his coach, I guided Sam through a process of intensive personal searching. Intensive personal searching represents Sam's independence: the need to step back and make conscious choices, by design, and live with them.

Independence is . . .

- knowing yourself and continuing your journey of self-discovery.
- choosing work that benefits you and others.
- feeling the freedom to change, and changing when you have grown beyond what you have been doing.

If We Take Care of Them (Do Our Job) They Will Take Care of Us

Too many of us have bought into the myth, "If we take care of them and do our job they will take care of us." Another rendition of this myth is, "They are my employers. I work *for* them. If I am loyal (in other words, dependent), they will be loyal to me (or, guarantee me a job)." People look to this as an anchor. When the anchor is tossed into rough seas, talented but dependent people go overboard. Experiencing and developing new beliefs will greatly enhance your chances for success and survival. One belief is that "nothing is permanent." Marianne, a biotech documentation specialist, *believed*, "I have to kill myself to make a decent living." She was working 75 hours a week. In her first consultation with me she asked, "Do I have the right skills for the job?" After listening to her stories about her successes, I determined that she had ample skills. I explained to Marianne, "Our skills alone do not determine our direction, feelings of success, and personal and professional development. They take a back seat to our beliefs, the rudder that steers our direction and quality of life." I asked Marianne, "What do you want to be different in your work, your life?" She said, "One thing is to work not more then 45 hours per week." Currently Marianne is examining her old beliefs, the ones that are no longer working. She is redefining her job and how she does it. She is also interviewing people who consult in her field to better understand what hours they work and how much they earn. These are steps toward adopting the new belief that she *can* work 45 hours a week, earn an income between $75,000 and $100,000, and have meaningful work. Following is a list of other typical beliefs and myths held by people in worklife transition and may curb independent efforts.

You Can Change Your Beliefs

Changing how you think is an essential part of the process of self-understanding. Your beliefs could be holding you back.

1. Myth: "If I change, I may fail."

   Empowered: Change is a natural part of living life.

2. Myth: Someone else will have the answer for me.

   Empowered: There is great joy in discovery; I can find or create the answer.

3. Myth: What my parents, spouse, and friends think is more important than what I think.

   Empowered: I will consider what others think as I formulate my own thoughts.

4. Myth: I'm too old [or too young] to change.

   Empowered: I can change at any age.

5. Myth: Other people get what they want, not me.

   Empowered: Understanding and articulating what I want is key to achieving my goals.

6. Myth: My work should satisfy all my needs.

   Empowered: Balance is important in my life. Satisfying work is part of that balance.

7. Myth: I shouldn't ask.

   Empowered: When I ask, I learn.

Don't Swim with a Full Stomach

How many times did your mother say, "Don't swim with a full stomach"? How many of you went swimming anyway? If you did, was the lifeguard called? Did you get cramps? Few, if any, of you, would answer "yes" to either question. If we don't try new things and ignore the wisdom of others, we will never know our own reality.

In the work world, it is as if too many workers have full stomachs and are afraid to swim. They continue to behave in detrimental, non-productive ways because of their attachment to past successes or to what someone told them, whether years ago or just yesterday. When people are dependent on another individual's thoughts, or on group-think, they eventually become afraid, lose hope, or never risk. Cindy, who had received her company's top design award, stopped taking risks. She lived with the message, "You've made it to the top. Why take a risk?" Pamela, a public relations executive, worked diligently for years to achieve her position and contribute to the company. Her new boss was also sexually harassing her. For months, despite her anguish, she told herself, "You've got a great job; you should be thankful." Eventually, she found support and challenged the myth that she should ignore the harassment. She confronted her boss, hired a lawyer, and won a lawsuit against her boss.

Interdependence

Whether you work in or outside of an organization, one-half of being self-employed is *in*dependence and the other half is *inter*dependence. Both require work to develop and maintain. Interdependence requires active thought plus deliberate *inter* action with others for the purpose of discussing problems, developing and testing ideas, formulating plans, and doing and perfecting work. Interdependence requires actively collaborating with and making a contribution to others—the organization, your customers, and your colleagues. At the same time, you are bridging—creating and maintaining—your independence and enhancing a clear sense of yourself. Like the shortstop on a baseball team, you are a key player, confident about your skill *and* in sync with your team's need.

Stop and think about a great baseball player. When he throws the ball to complete a spectacular double play, I doubt that he feels he is giving up anything. He is using his *individual* strength as a component of the *team's* strength. Similarly, when workers are exempted from being part of a team or they feel left out, they don't have a chance to use their skills and make a contribution to the team. When they do participate they are passing on their strength and making a contribution to others.

Interdependence is rooted in equality (openness and sharing) not subordination (fear and manipulation). Some of my clients, whether management or staff, have figuratively merged with the company they work "for" (dependence); they have no sense of working "with" the organization (independence and interdependence). They have lost their selfness—who they are, separate from the organization. Laid off from her software engineering position, Juanita felt confused but relieved. "The buyout," she said, "gave me a chance to explore who I am and what I want independent of the company. I was doing whatever my bosses requested, whether I believed in a project or not. I began to see the stark difference between the culture I had come from and the culture that the company was becoming. I realized that during the past seven years, *I* had been bought out! My dependence on the company had ruined my self-confidence."

Interdependence is...

▤ collaborating with and supporting others.

▤ trusting others to support you.

▤ working toward a goal that challenges you and contributes to your workplace, community, and customers.

We cannot escape the connectedness of the world, not least because the more we concentrate on what we are best at, the more we will need the expertise of others. Self-sufficiency is an idle dream. Even those who cultivate their own organic plots need trucks built by others to drive their produce to market along roads maintained by others.

—*Charles Handy, The Hungry Spirit*

More than One Boss or Customer

In my counseling and coaching work I wouldn't think of depending on one client, individual, or organization for my income. First, this is a form of dependence, and in my business I believe dependence is unethical. If I were dependent in my work, I'd be holding onto my clients rather than encouraging their mobility and increasing their productivity. Second, having more than one boss (client) is fascinating and fun. I'm curious. I learn from my clients. What they give to me, I give to other clients, and we all move together toward success. Ming, a management and leadership consultant, said, "In my work, I am not only helping clients to manage change but also to *cause* change. I work with executives, for instance, who are reshaping their companies. Many of these companies are profitable, but today's executives know they can't simply rest on past success. They must learn new skills and attitudes." Ming expanded and reinforced my thinking. I use her notion with *my* clients and now I'm sharing it with you.

If you work at a company, work within as many departments and with as many bosses as you can. If you consult to organizations or coach individuals, expand. Select a variety of clients from various backgrounds and industries. Your life will be richer and so will theirs. And don't forget that when clients terminate, or your company reorganizes, or your boss is terminated, you'll go on to have other clients, companies, and bosses.

Are you dependent—the old employee-employer contract—or are you negotiating an independent and interdependent path? The following chart will help you see the difference and learn how to make choices.

Dependence or Independence and Interdependence

Seeing the options before you and actively thinking about them is that first step toward choosing between dependence and independence/interdependence. The left column below shows 10 primary characteristics of dependence. The right column shows the 10 corresponding independent/interdependent characteristics. As you read each dependent characteristic and compare it to its independent/interdependent characteristic, think about and write down on a piece of paper the characteristic that best describes the way you currently see yourself.

Dependent	Independent and Interdependent
I seek and wait for approval before committing to action.	I give myself permission to contribute.
I resist new ideas and leave creativity to others.	I create new ideas, options, and projects.
First, I am loyal to my company and customers.	First, I am loyal to myself. If I meet my needs, I can give to others.
I ignore my inner voice. Instead, I put my fate in others' hands.	I listen to and respect my wisdom; I incorporate my knowing into my decision making.
I rarely give thought to matters; mostly I react to conditions.	I engage in active thought and deliberate action.
I keep information to myself.	I readily share information with others.
I am driven by company and client expectations.	I offer my opinions and respect those of others.
Most of the time, I suppress who I am—sublimate my passion and compromise my values.	I strive to understand and appreciate what I have to contribute and share in a common purpose.
I am apt to manipulate the system—find underhanded ways to get my needs met.	I view myself as resourceful; I negotiate with others to achieve my goals.
Basically, I work for a paycheck.	I work to make a contribution, and I am paid for performance.

On a piece of paper, write down one of your dependent characteristics. Make it a goal over the next month to become conscious of your thoughts and behavior in this area. Follow through: become more independent and interdependent by discussing with a colleague some ways that you can change your behavior. Barney, a lawyer, felt that the fourth dependent characteristic was inhibiting his progress at work. He wrote, "Too often I ignore my inner voice. I defer to the opinions of others."

After a discussion with a friend, Barney decided to take some action steps. He stated them affirmatively.

Barney's Action Steps:

I will...

- ▤ take 15 minutes every day to think about what is important to me.
- ▤ not judge my solutions to work problems. First, I will write them down and discuss them with a colleague I trust.
- ▤ make a point, at least once or twice a week, to share my opinions with my boss and colleagues.

Think of one of the dependent characteristics you recorded and name three actions you might take toward independence and interdependence.

Serve Yourself to Serve Your Clients and Yourself

Several of my clients are mid-level managers in large corporations who are still gainfully employed. Many have been struggling to survive, trying to adapt to organizations they joined five, ten, or twenty-five years ago that are today unrecognizable. Their jobs are unlikely to last. Some want to learn to manage their careers and find or create new jobs within their company. Others are feeling, for personal reasons, that it is time for them to explore options outside of their company—to think beyond what is familiar, to consider their own needs and what they want to contribute to others in the next stage of their lives. This process of giving up familiar territory, overcoming obstacles, and identifying options is painfully difficult for most. They are seeking my support, guidance, and expertise.

One client, Michael, manager of compensation for the division of an automobile manufacturer, called one afternoon with a request. "I'd like to ask you a favor which at first may sound strange." Michael asked if I would call his voice mail at work and leave a supportive message. The message would contain positive, encouraging statements that Michael had heard me use to describe him in past sessions. Michael's ability to know what he needs and to summon the courage to ask for it is unusual and admirable. Particularly for men, asking for help is difficult because it is often interpreted as a weakness. I left Michael this message:

> Michael,
> I want you to truly hear—absorb—this message about you. The most important thing you can do for yourself and for others is to express your authentic self. This means go for win/win, share your ideas, and listen to others; be a coach—you're a natural at this; use your creativity—you have wonderfully innovative and practical ideas. Delegate responsibility—this is your way of trusting others; don't worry about your competence—you're an expert in your field. Mostly, Michael, serve yourself to serve your clients and yourself.

Once he became aware of it, Michael (and many others with whom I work) discovered that he feared his dependence on the organization. Many of us are uncertain about how much of our competence is ours and how much can be attributed to the organization and others. As a result, we may feel despair and gravely question our ability to work in another organization or to make some other type of career change. To feel independent and act interdependently, we must free ourselves from years of brainwashing with the "serve the company and we'll serve you" notion. It is anguishing to sift through and wrestle with old messages and expectations. It is challenging and often lonely to go to work and quietly sort through the noise, internally and externally, in order to hear your own voice. If you are fortunate enough to hear it, respect and follow it.

Ask a friend to leave you a voice mail message.
Dial it often. Sit back, take it in.

The Yogurt Man was a Self-Leader

Wherever I go, I make a point to notice how people do their work. One day at the grocery store, I was heading up the dairy aisle to buy a half-gallon of milk. I spotted a clerk quietly stacking yogurt containers. Gingerly, he turned each one so the brand name was in clear customer view, then placed one more on top of the first and again turned the label to the front. The man calmly completed his eye-catching display with impeccable order. The small containers stretched seven rows across and five levels high.

I said to him, "That's quite a job." He responded, "Yes, it is. Thanks for noticing." The yogurt man was relaxed and seemed to accept himself. He likes his job. He gives meaning to it. As I completed my shopping, I was struck by the personal and organizational value the man brought to his job. He was, in fact, a "customer," treating each container as if he were going to buy it. I also thought about the value of his work to me, the customer, and to his organization, another customer.

The yogurt man was a self-leader, taking charge of his worklife. He exhibited independence (he knew himself) and interdependence (he collaborated with and contributed to others). It seemed he believed he was running his own business within a business. He took responsibility for his satisfaction and passed it on to his customers and organization. I imagined that to run his own business within a business, he likely collaborates effectively with his boss, vendors, and colleagues. No one can sustain and succeed while operating in a cocoon. Interdependence, or creating and maintaining relationships, is as important as independence, or knowing and utilizing your assets. Imagine them as pivotal gears that, when engaged, you lead by taking charge, progressing, and adding value to others.

Whether you stack shelves, teach or manage others, or run a business, the world around you will continue to change and turn upside-down. As well, you'll personally feel the need to grow and seek new opportunities. To thrive today, you must be like the yogurt man and work "with" your organization as a self-leader—independently and interdependently—to continually enhance your abilities and contributions to the whole.

Be Aware of the Great Jackass Fallacy

"The dominant philosophy of motivation in American management is the 'carrot-and-stick philosophy: reward and punishment,'" writes Harry Levinson, management consultant and professor, in *The Great Jackass Fallacy*. "The first image that comes to mind when one thinks 'carrot-and-stick' is a jackass," Dr. Levinson writes, "Obviously the unconscious assumption behind the reward and punishment model is that one is dealing with jackasses, that people are to be manipulated and controlled. Thus, unconsciously, the boss is the manipulator and controller, and the subordinate is the jackass." If you feel like a jackass long enough, you begin to act like one—stubborn. You consciously or unconsciously come to work late, miss deadlines, blame others, and/or stop volunteering. At this point, you have a chance to reframe "stubborn" as your need for independence and interdependence. Independence and interdependence, in this case, does not mean leaving the company and closing the books on your clients or customers. It does, however, refer to the reassessment of your power—your mental and physical ability to stop thinking and acting like a jackass and to begin confronting the obstacles that block your independent thought and interdependent action.

You No Longer Work *For*, You Work *With*

Even in a work world filled with jackasses, you can work *with*, not *for*, a company. Again, *with* implies equality and dignity and the ability to respond to challenges *as well as* to respect others. If you are someone who works *for*, you frequently expect direction and ask your boss, "What do you want me to do?" By contrast, it is empowering to work *with* your boss or *with* a team. Your language might change to "I'd like to suggest this as a next step" or "I can identify the problem and, although I don't have any answers yet, I'd like to volunteer to do some research." If you are leading a team, you could work *with* by saying, "I've learned to trust your individual expertise and ability to contribute. As we divvy up responsibilities for our next project, I'd like each of you to think about and discuss openly how you might contribute." You might even find that your physical posture changes as well!

With makes a statement about your interdependence. It says, "I've joined the team as a participant in pursuit of a common purpose." *With* is also a statement about your independence. It says, "This is what I have to offer." *With* is a link to the team, project, or organization. It is also a safety net and path toward other opportunities. With is your new reality.

It is a mistake for people to think that they truly work *for* anyone. "At my last job," commented Erik, an engineer, "I believed that I worked for myself and that I was associated *with* the company. In thinking this way, I felt freer to do my work without preoccupation: What if the company downsizes? Will my job be eliminated?" Instead, Erik has learned to value working with the company, doing what needs to be done to serve his customers and colleagues and attending to his own developmental needs.

In our parish, the Unitarian Universalist Church of Arlington, Massachusetts, Barbara Whittacker-Johns, the senior minister, is *called* to the parish. That is, she works with us as an independent and interdependent contractor. She fills out her own 1099! Barbara's independence fosters stimulating, sometimes controversial, and always thought provoking sermons. The pulpit is not controlled by a dependent—*for*—mentality (We've *hired* you). And Barbara exhibits and utilizes her interdependence as she talks with members, gathers opinions, offers pastoral care, and shares her leadership spirit: collaboration with our community.

I deal everyday with people's struggles about dependence on the organization they work *for*. As we have seen, dependent people say, "I have no idea what I would do without my job," "I'd love to leave, but what else would I do?" and "At least I have a job." A dependent business owner might say, "I'll do anything to keep my customers" or "I'll never find another worker like Mike." In part, dependence is common because people do not see or learn that there are alternatives and that they do have power.

I grew up believing that truth conquers all and I still follow this maxim. The practical and liberating alternative to dependence combines independence with interdependence. You can be your own person and be part of a team. Remember the flock of migrating geese? Even though others may be tuned in to a dependence frequency or wired to the beat of someone else's music, you don't have to be.

Internal Hierarchies

Over the years, many of us have developed the necessary muscles—intellectual, emotional, and physical—for negotiating hierarchical or superior-subordinate relationships. The same narrow, top-down arrangement exists internally as well as externally. It is expressed in our self-talk. For example, "First is better," "Ask permission before you try," and "Fight at any cost to reach the top." Passed on and reinforced by our working predecessors, internalized hierarchies are not easy to examine. We must challenge and rearrange the framework of "carrots and sticks"—rewards and punishments.

Our parents reminded us to "be good." Our teachers said, "If you raise your hand first with the *right* answer, you'll be rewarded." Our bosses insisted, "If you do what you're told and deliver, you'll be paid." Our internal hierarchies reflect what we have been taught—dependence on a system. We are controlled by the notion of reward and punishment. I've had clients say to me, "If I'm not promoted, I'll leave," as if there were no other choices. Like dependent children, they pout. Some even run away.

The hierarchy also keeps us focused on the organization's mission and goals, with little attention to our own. Who has the time to attend to—much less reward us for—our goals? "Competition was the name of the game, but one day, I woke up to my needs," commented Jill, a territory sales supervisor. "Now I job-share with Sandra, another supervisor. We each work part time."

Self-Control

Narrow, rigid hierarchies fed by unbridled growth have depended predominantly on the wisdom of the "superiors." In these uncharted times, the economic, spiritual, and physical fate of individuals and organizations can no longer be placed into the hands of superiors. Their strength may be admirable and helpful, but alone it is limiting. The involvement and contribution of others—your vision and expertise—have become essential. "I'm a 'utility player,'" said Melanie, a systems analyst. "I go where the problems are and use my abilities to manage, lead, and implement. I used to see myself as someone who would do anything necessary to climb the stovepipe to the top. The company that I worked *for* reinforced this and I bought in. My MBA served as a competitive weapon. The company has been slow to change, but today it seems they respect my versatility more and I feel liberated by my awareness that other organizations might also need my skills."

For Melanie, self-control replaced being controlled. Internally, she replaced the image of climbing a stovepipe with that of ascending a willow tree—well rooted, distinctive, and flexible. She is able to grow, stand firm, bend, and sway. Her MBA is no longer a weapon but a symbolic reminder of her ability to learn and to continue learning. It's a source of self-confidence and gives her cache in the marketplace.

Andre, a training coordinator with talent and passion in the applied arts, was still blocked by the traditional ladder—*in his mind*. When he talked about turning his artistic talents into a business he initially glowed. But then he asked, "Who would buy my work? There are a lot of great artists out there. A few make money; most don't." I said, "Yes, there are great artists out there and, like you, they have to learn, first, to recognize *their* greatness. Then, the possibility of making money is enhanced. Among other things, this will take quieting the societal noise and listening to and nurturing more of your inner voice."

Listed below are different ways we think about our work. As you can see, the statements in the left column illustrate some rigid, dependent ways of thinking. In the right column, the statements show more flexibility and independence. Note the statements that most accurately reflect your beliefs. Be careful not to judge yourself as you review your answers. Use this exercise as a learning tool.

It's important to...

▤ be first.	▤ be involved.
▤ move up.	▤ move in the direction of your joy and make a contribution.
▤ know the answer.	▤ know and ask questions.
▤ ask the boss.	▤ seek another's opinion, not permission.
▤ change only when necessary.	▤ continually look at alternatives, explore, and experiment.
▤ be rewarded.	▤ be rewarded and reward yourself.

If you're willing to risk and accept responsibility, you can have equality and dignity.

You can...

▤ speak your mind, volunteer solutions, and initiate conversation and meetings.

▤ prioritize your values and live them.

▤ rewrite your job description and apply for or create a new job.

▤ use your abilities in a different company.

▤ become your own boss—you are anyway.

▤ develop new services and sell to different customers.

▤ analyze what makes you a top performer.

▤ set new goals and enjoy the process as you achieve them.

▤ create a whole new worklife.

Integrating independence and interdependence takes effort, and it works. It starts, evolves, and continues with you.

Lemons into Lemonade: One Person Makes a Difference

A commercial real estate firm I call Hartman and Clark was structured hierarchically. Workers at all levels had bosses and the bosses had the answers. It was a dependent worker system. Today they have hired a consulting firm to guide the executives through a culture change—a process that will flatten the company and change the ways people think and work. This process involves assembling workers into teams of specialists—experts collaborating with one another to improve service to customers. Hartman and Clark will soon be an interdependent workplace. The company's reorganization effort is aimed at creating a new, nonhierarchical structure in which all workers are responsible for their individual productivity *and* their team's productivity. A revised compensation plan will reflect the change: individuals will be paid a salary and each team will receive a bonus based on performance.

Clive, one of the senior partners, called me and said, "We have a couple of people in the firm who have been valuable players, but I'm *not* sure if they can change as our organization does. I'm not convinced that they need to go; that's why I'm calling you. I want to change this company *and* help people to make changes *with* us." We met and decided that I would begin coaching Anthony, a financial analyst who had been with the firm for several years. Clive thought Anthony might have difficulty adapting to the team approach.

First I interviewed Brent, Anthony's boss. Brent summarized Anthony's problem: "He's just not an effective team player." Surprisingly, in my initial conversation with Anthony, he saw doing some "career work" as an opportunity, one he had thought about in the past but needed a push to act on. Anthony liked his job and felt that he was well suited to his role. Regarding cultural fit, he remarked, "Most of the people in my division are more expressive than I am—they are sales types. I like to work *alone* on projects to get the job done. I also like to think that my work speaks for itself, unlike my colleagues, who frequently announce, 'Look what I just accomplished.'" Toward the close of our meeting I assured Anthony that he would learn a great deal from the coaching process and that I would be supportive of him. "Anthony," I said, "you will build your confidence and you will be able make sense of information that can be very helpful as you make choices and changes."

Our plan for Anthony included taking two career inventories, the Myers-Briggs Type Indicator (MBTI) and the Johnson O'Connor Inventory of Aptitudes and Knowledge (JOIAK). The MBTI gives people information about their personality type, which can be used to make effective career or job decisions and help people better understand their communication style. The JOIAK helps people discover or affirm their aptitudes or natural talents (musical and artistic talents are examples of aptitudes).

After completing the inventories, Anthony received feedback from each diagnostic specialist on my team. Anthony invited Kim, his wife, to join him at our meetings. She provided support, and her own experience with Anthony affirmed some of the observations we had made. In my practice, every client who sits across from me is not sitting alone. Each has a *worklife*—a larger, interconnected system. As Anthony sat across from me during our first meeting I was aware that his wife, children, parents, boss, other people in his life, past and present, as well as societal expectations and mortgage payments, were also present and influencing his choices and behavior. This is the case for all of us: even when we are alone, we are not alone.

Anthony discovered that his aptitude with numbers and tonal memory lent themselves naturally to his work with facts and figures—

validation for what he already knew. He learned through the MBTI that his natural tendency was to relate more to the inner world of ideas (introversion) rather than to the outer world of people (extraversion). Kim, an extravert, pointed out that she had reminded him of this fact several times throughout their marriage. His introverted nature, although different from many in his division, did not make him better or worse than others, just different. And Anthony's style was part of what he uniquely brought to his team. His task was to learn how to communicate more effectively with his colleagues so that he would be understood and their needs would be met. As Anthony said, most of his team members preferred to talk frequently about their accomplishments. Different communication styles didn't mean they weren't a team; they still had a common purpose—to serve the customer. Anthony learned that he could communicate with them and respect his own, more inward style by writing and e-mailing a weekly update memo to each team member.

Anthony said, "I was dealt a handful of lemons, and I'm turning them into lemonade for myself and others." Clarifying his personality type and confirming his aptitudes demonstrated to Anthony the power of knowing himself (an ongoing process) in a changing system. He did not have to be a victim; he could become a player again.

With encouragement from his wife, renewed spirit, and with clarification and new words to explain his attributes, Anthony arranged a meeting with Clive and Brent. He thanked Clive and Brent for the opportunity to learn about himself, told them what he learned and what the process involved, and proposed that they encourage others to go through the same process. Following this meeting, Clive and Brent made a commitment to support other individuals in the organization to learn about their communication styles. Their aim was to help Anthony's colleagues benefit from increased self-knowledge too, and then apply that knowledge to working more productively together. With a more aware and functional team of workers, Clive and Brent could now expect to see increased revenues.

Clive and Brent learned that the notion of having a "perfect" team of clones is not the answer to the need for improved productivity. It is at best a temporary solution. Changing team members, a fluctuating marketplace, and increasing competition call for flexible, multi-skilled teams. The knowledge that workers at Hartman and Clark gained about their aptitudes and communication styles gave them personal power to make changes and helped them communicate more effectively with one another. Good teams have members with complementary skills who respect one another's differences.

Successful "organizational" redeveloping cannot occur without "personal" redeveloping—people learning to become more independent and interdependent. That's where Anthony, Hartman and Clark, and the world of work are headed. We are all taking responsibility for discovering who we are and making a contribution to others.

Career/Job Enhancement, Not Only Advancement

Career/job enhancement is an ongoing process of self-development, career planning, productivity, and contribution that neither precludes nor depends on career/job advancement. The traditional career ladder is the obvious career/job advancement choice but, as we have discussed earlier, now that organizations are flattening, the ladder approach is less available. The concept of enhancement puts the onus on you to question your purpose do your skills inventory, notice the needs in your organization, and identify your customer's needs. If you choose enhancement, you will be challenged rather than restricted by the limits of advancement. You will actively seek opportunities.

As you enhance, you are likely to advance. If you choose enhancement, you will challenge the "one-boss advancement" model. "I used to accept a new job because I believed in the boss and because the advancement opportunities looked good," said Gary, director of quality control at a hospital. "Basically, I trusted my boss and behaved as though he would pull me up the ladder as he was promoted." Gary's career values have shifted. "Today, I look at the bigger picture. My boss was fired and so was I. Looking back, I hadn't gotten involved enough. I knew only a small circle of people and focused on doing the tasks that I thought would give me visibility [promotions]." Dependence, as illustrated by Gary's singular focus on advancement, is a vulnerable state. If something happened to your boss or your career track, what would you do?

By identifying contacts in or outside of your organization, you can collect important information—company goals, new product reviews, job leads—for your career enhancement. Your task, after writing down some names, is to network or gather information. Networking is the active development and careful use of contacts for personal and professional development. It is not for the purpose of job interviewing. Some of my clients complain that many company contacts are refusing to grant informational interviews, and I suspect the reason is partially that job seekers have become more manipulative—they ask for one thing but do another.

Self-Respect: A Case Study

"My boss might ask me to do 20 things, and I might get 19 of them right," said Jolienne, a compensation specialist. "She then berates me for my one mistake. This happens constantly. I know it's not just me—she scolds other staff in the same way. The longer I stay at my job, the more I'm losing respect for myself." When I asked Jolienne why she had not done something to change her situation, she initially said it was because she had a three-year-old son and this part-time job allowed her to spend time with him. Ultimately, she uncovered a deeper reason. She believed it would be nearly impossible to find a part-time job in her field, let alone one she would enjoy.

I asked Jolienne if she had ever experienced other, similar conflicts. She had—at a previous job and in her relationship with her mother. "In my old job, I grew intolerant of my supervisor's put-downs and packed my bags. Regarding my mother, I was the one in my family to challenge her criticisms; my brother and sister would sit back while I'd talk back. It didn't do much good [and] to this day my mother still criticizes us. So I handle the situation by visiting my parents as little as possible, maybe once or twice a year."

Jolienne doubted that her worklife could be different, that she could choose a boss who would encourage her and treat her with dignity. I said, "You can have your doubts, but please leave a little opening for the possibility that you can become independent and choose healthier work relationships." She began to recognize the ways that she had become dependent on—grown accustomed to—a demeaning type of relationship. In addition, she was able to identify times when she *had* chosen healthier relationships, ones in which she had reached internally for *her* inner voice and preserved her dignity by speaking up.

Over time, Jolienne talked more about her doubts and her unhealthy relationships, as well as her positive choices. She began to deepen her understanding of what was important to her and what to look for in other people. For example, she had strong intuitive skills and claimed she could sense the type of boss who would not be a good match for her. She didn't always trust her intuition, however. I asked, "Would you give me an example of something your current boss says or does that you would characterize as demeaning?" Jolienne responded, "She says things like, 'Do it. I don't want any questions' or she will ask, 'What do you think?' but then walk away as I'm answering. Or, she will constantly say, 'I want you to ask me before you do anything.'"

Eventually, Jolienne reframed the negative message, "I can't trust my intuition." She called her intuition "my best friend; someone I can trust." "A best friend," she declared, "listens. Sometimes they say nothing at all, but their presence gives me courage and faith in myself." I asked her, "Is there anyone in your life who depends on your intuition?" She said, "My son. When he cries, I just know what he needs." "What do you mean?" "I trust [listen to] my intuition!"

Next Jolienne began to think of several situations at work when she had trusted her intuition. She had offered a troubled colleague timely help, for example, and once she choose the name for one of the company's new products. I then asked her, "When you think of times when your intuition has been your 'best friend,' how did you behave? What would I see you doing?" "I asked people questions, volunteered solutions, and actually did things to advance the project," she responded. "Often I was first to come up with new ideas." "When you did not trust you intuition, how did you behave?" "I kept to myself," Jolienne reflected.

Reframing Changes Behavior

Old Frame	Reframe
Thought: I can't trust my intuition.	My intuition is my best friend.
Behavior: Withdraws, closes down.	Contributes, questions, volunteers solutions.

While Jolienne was in the process of looking for another job, I continued to encourage her to take on a "self-employed" attitude—to integrate independence (clarify what she needed) and interdependence (understand the needs and operative style of a boss and team that she might be joining). She gradually learned to honor her intuitive perception, ask pointed questions, and listen acutely to the response. In one interview she asked a prospective boss, "Would you give me several examples of how you work with your staff?" Notice she did not say, "Would you tell me about the times when you have *collaborated* with your staff?" This might have cued her interviewer about her *own* values, something she would share later in the interview. The neutral question allows for a more objective answer. When Jolienne finally found a new part-time position, she had not only interviewed the boss but the staff as well. She did not ask the staff if their boss was fair, open, direct, or flexible. Instead, she asked staff members to describe the ways in which the boss operated. Again, it was critical not to indicate any bias in her inquiry; she gave the staff minimal cues about what she was looking for in order to elicit responses she could trust.

Jolienne learned to think and act independently and eventually found a work situation in which interdependent relationships prevailed, including the one between her and her boss.

Signs that You are Integrating Independence and Interdependence

You are developing...

- an ability to move beyond your fears.
- a loyalty to "self-truth."
- a sense that you can make a difference.
- a willingness to plan and risk.
- a facility to manage outcomes.
- a spirit of adventure.
- a gracious attitude toward others on their journey.
- a loss of interest in controlling others.
- a freedom to give and receive.

Move Closer to Your Independence and Interdependence

Early in the morning on Columbus Day, 1993, I looked across Memorial Drive to the Charles River. Suddenly a bullet-shaped car with a one-seat cockpit sped by, soon followed by a vehicle with flashing lights. I guessed that the "bullet" car must have been experimental and that it was probably heading three miles up the road to its birthplace, the Massachusetts Institute of Technology (MIT).

"How appropriate," I thought, "that on our holiday for celebrating discovery, innovators were pioneering and testing a new and unusual vehicle." I imagined that the experimental car was a result of a team effort and that each of the inventors had courage, imagination, and a spirit of adventure. Each had taken on a responsibility to invent something new—to discover and test a different way of doing something. Most likely, the inventors had each challenged conventional wisdom—their own and others'. This team of individuals (independent) had come together for a common purpose (interdependent). While watching this car on its test run, I saw the initial result of a collective effort. Back then I thought, "Someday, you may be buying the final result!"

Such inventors work independently, *with* MIT and *with* one another. It is amazing what individuals can do when their intention is clear, they know themselves, and they take responsibility for harnessing individual and team energy. They overcome inner and outer obstacles and persevere to make what they have imagined a reality. They work authentically, collaboratively, and productively from their passion and purpose. They are discovering new frontiers and stretching beyond what others may never have thought was humanly possible.

As you learn to become more independent and interdependent you will gain greater satisfaction and yield more productivity from your work. You will feel more alive—lighter and happier. In the next chapter you will discover that working *with* others defies gravity and is at the core of this notion.

Who's the Boss?
Check-In: Integrating Independence and Interdependence

1. Is there a time when you have been *dependent*—constrained by another or your own feelings and behaviors, or unrealistically expectant that someone else would have the answer for you? What resulted? How did you feel?

2. When have you been *independent*—trusted your own skill and/or intuition? What resulted? How did you feel?

3. When have you been *interdependent*—collaborated with, and contributed to, others? What resulted? How did you feel?

4. What is a myth, or dependent belief, that you might hold? (For example, "Others are more able to change than me.") What is a more empowered, or productive, belief that you could adopt?

5. Who might you ask to leave you an encouraging voice mail or e-mail that you could refer to at any time? Access it often. Sit back, take it in.

WORKING WITH, NOT FOR, YOUR ORGANIZATION AND CUSTOMERS

*Do work and build relationships based on respect,
equality, and competence.*

EMPLOYED ATTITUDE
Dependent Mindset

I am enmeshed with the organization and customers; I work for them.
Whether I agree or not, I always do what is expected of me.

SELF-EMPLOYED ATTITUDE
Independent and Interdependent Mindset

I think about my values, respect the values of others, and look for the
right time to voice my opinion. I provide service-based equality and
competence, whether I work inside or outside the organization.

When I recall my most enjoyable and productive work experiences, I think of times I felt strongly about what I was doing and when I was working with peers. Peers are those with whom I have an equal relationship and for whom I have great respect. Peer work occurs when you join with a person or an organization for a shared purpose—a joint venture of equals. We listen and are listened to, we share our ideas and consider the ideas of others, we give constructive criticism and receive feedback from others, and everyone maintains his or her dignity in the process. I had that experience while writing this book. After I wrote the first draft the publisher, Berrett-Koehler, and I sent copies to several reviewers. Although I did not know most of the reviewers, I considered their feedback and the care they put into formulating their comments an invaluable peer review. Each reviewer wrote a comprehensive letter describing what she or he would keep and change in the manuscript.

Ralph Katz, a friend and colleague, was one of the reviewers. Ralph questioned the original subject of this chapter, the notion of "partnering" with your organization. Ralph felt that for most workers today the notion of partnering was rigid, too permanent. He challenged me to think in terms of *peer* relationships and their influence on healthy working relationships. After careful thought, I revised the chapter to include

Ralph's suggestion. Thanks in part to my peer relationship with him, this chapter explores some thoughts about peer work and ways it could work for you.

Peer Work

Peer work—working with others for a shared purpose—is built on the fundamental requirement of equality. Few of us want to feel "less than" another person (a boss) with whom we work. Most of us want to be able to share our ideas, work with others toward common goals, and have respect and equality in the process. We want to establish this peer relationship with our fellow workers, suppliers, and customers.

The clients I work with who are most fulfilled enjoy this kind of relationship with their organization, customers, and colleagues while working toward a goal. They make contributions using their authentic selves in the process and in return are challenged, recognized, and rewarded. They benefit from joint satisfaction gained over a period of time.

Peer work entails an ongoing process of learning, negotiating, and contributing. A finished project becomes a catalyst toward deeper relationships and future opportunities. Two consultants, for example, co-authored an article and are now working on a book. Peer work, in addition, drives the creation of my Rethinking Work® newsletter and my ongoing learning from and contribution to others. I ask a client or colleague to join me to become the "inspiring interview," the feature story, for each issue. Wendy Martin, a lead singer and songwriter and office manager for Fortune Small Business joined me for the December 2002 issue, *Never Have Regrets.* I asked Wendy about True to Life, her upcoming one-woman play. "In our initial conversation you said it's about 'accepting who you are.' And you went on to say, 'It's about facing life head on and learning from it and about yourself.' This is scary stuff for many people. How do you 'face life head on?'"

Wendy said, "When I say 'face life head on' I mean you need to accept who you are, where you came from, who your family is, what you have endured. You can never run away from anything, nor can you deny it. Scary? Hell yeah. Very scary! Facing scary stuff sometimes hurts others and I think that can be the hardest part about it. But that type of pain can heal because it's honest, real pain. It's not a symptom of other stuff or from a past circumstance. I'm still trying to acknowledge and learn what my symptoms are and where they came from so not to project them onto other people, especially children.

"I remember one day sitting in front of the TV watching the Ms. America pageant with my two nieces, Molly and Alicia, when all of sudden Molly screamed. 'I got the best idea Aunt Wendy, you should be Ms. America!' I remember all of us laughing because Molly really thought she hit a gold mine with that one. A week or so went by and I went back to my waitress job and told all my friends (actors, dancers, singers, painters, poets, etc.), the story of Molly and from that day forward I was referred to as "Ms. America." Although the story prompted a lot of laughs, it also made me realize that these kids, my nieces, idolized me. At that time I was a very dark person, basically, very confused and unhappy. I felt a great responsibility to be a good role model for them and I knew the only way to do that was to be true to myself and take responsibility for myself. This was another juncture to making a new ending, and beginning, for my life.

Following are words from the song "When Molly Said…" by Wendy Martin.

Molly girl, you will see
The swimsuit talent is not for me.

I'm more inclined to sign petitions
Then try to win a competition.

But if they'd ask me, "What I'd do,
If I could change the world for You?"

I'd tell them that I'd spend my life
Making sure you'll be alright.
I'd tell them that I learned from life
To try and change what is not right!

Starlight, Starbright
I wish I may, I wish I might
Be the one to be forthright
And bring about the honest truth
Instead of yesterday's excuse.

—*Wendy Martin*

Just before the newsletter was published I met Wendy for breakfast. One topic of discussion was her prolific ability to tell stories. I suggested that when she sang in front of her audiences that between songs, she lace in her stories. A few months later, I received the following note.

I had a very big gig in December, more like a Holiday party. I sang many "requested" songs to all the people I love in my life and told stories of our friendship and what they mean to me. You gave me this idea...it was a huge success.

Wendy

The rewards of peer work are priceless.

Working with each other does *not* mean drafting a document that requires a two-party signature or a debate over whose name will appear in larger print. Peer work is a joint activity undertaken by two or more people with common interests, mutual respect, and goals that lead to effective outcomes. It is a *process* rather than a legal structure and it is possible to create with others, at different levels, in your organization. Working with your organization in today's scrutinizing and cost-conscious work climate—where at any time you could be viewed as an asset or a liability—requires wisdom, hard work, and patience.

One of my clients, Annette, a senior director of strategic management for a large pharmaceutical company, was told by her boss Burt that she would have her performance review in one week. Annette said, "I don't mind the review process, but the way it's done 'according to Burt' bothers me. I don't like going into Burt's office and taking the chair in front of his desk while he sits back in the chair behind his desk. Right away, before he says a word, I feel subordinated, as though he has most of the power and I'm left with little." I asked Annette, "What do you think that you might do that could shift the balance in this situation? We both know that your job isn't to change Burt!"

In a few moments, Annette looked at me with wide-open eyes. She said, "I've got it! I'll ask Burt to meet me at the coffee shop across the street. We could meet after the morning crowd...there's usually a private table in the corner available." I asked, "Why the coffee shop?" "Because," Annette said, "this setting would take Burt out of his office space. We'd sit across from each other, no desk between us, like peers. I'd feel less intimidated, more able to listen and respond to what he's said and offer my opinions, too."

My brother Chris, a rheumatologist, runs a peer practice. He serves his patients by actively listening and learning from them. Chris and his staff share their ideas and observations to deliver quality service. Linda, an Olympics hopeful, swims laps most days of the year. Her coach encourages and guides her. They work together, always with the goal that Linda will qualify for the Olympics in mind. In a corporate retail setting, Herb, a senior merchandise manager, believes, "You have to build bridges with people and find a common ground. You must ask yourself, 'What kinds of relationships am I creating?' The win is in the interpersonal win, it's in the trust...bonding [peer] relationships as you are employed."

Page 149 shows a comparison between the essential elements of working for (subordinating yourself) and working with (peer work).

Reframing the Way You Work

At this point you might be thinking, "Peer work, where I work, between me and my company? Impossible!" But I am not talking about a partnership—a formal title and position. I am suggesting joining—a flexible, expansive activity in which you think in terms of possibilities, engage in problem solving, and commit to going ahead. "Going ahead" is an hour-to-hour decision for some. For others it is a daily ritual to put their best effort into whatever job they are doing. You could be looking for a job, redefining your current job, addressing a customer's complaint, or figuring out how to launch your company's next product. Joining is a component of your "self-employed" attitude whereby you overcome your resistance to change and involve yourself in the business at hand. You do not allow yourself to be pulled downstream; you use your imagination, values, energy, and skill to solve problems—swim ahead—and become part of the solution.

✖

Sometimes your imagination carries you.
—Gabriella Hakim

Sometimes, You Grapple

Peer work sometimes takes grappling with your values and with others. You naturally want an easy answer, but instead, you must wrestle with your ambivalence, wait, and see what happens. Ricky, a communications specialist, said, "Cliff, for some 'political' reason [my colleague] Jack thinks I should make a donation to Alpha-Med (fictitious company name); that is become a 'friend of Alpha-Med.' He is on the development committee. Jack got me this work. They are my main client and main means of support...Does the consultant commonly make a donation to the client? I told Jack it felt like a payoff. What do you think?"

I responded, "Ricky, I'm not sure that what I think is so important in this situation. I know you to have strong ethical values...you'll likely do what you feel is the right thing to do." After thinking about my response over night, Ricky said, "I'm going to stand my ground. Making a donation would go against my ethics and compromise the objectivity that I have with my client." Making the donation would have subordinated Ricky; instead, she chose to work *with* her client.

Are You Working For or With?

Compare the column on the left with the one on the right and note the behavior that best describes what you do. Remember, seeing your current behavior can become a springboard for change.

Working For *Subordinating Yourself*	*Joining* *Peer Work*
Looking "up" for direction and most of the answers.	Questioning, collaborating, and negotiating with others to discover common ground and develop solutions.
Staying put when feeling apathetic about company values, services, and/or products.	Owning your own values and feeling genuinely aligned with the company's vision and goals.
Accepting and doing the same repetitive work.	Learning new processes and contributing to colleagues and customers.
Waiting for others to plan your worklife.	Initiating and continuing your personal and professional growth.
Seeing others primarily as a boss and/or a competitor.	Creating relationships built on mutual and/or a respect and common purpose, support, and the exchange of information and ideas.

Work With Others—Join In—for Individual Mobility and Organizational Productivity

It is a false premise that any organization can retain its best workers: as if people and events can be manipulated and success guaranteed so long as the company keeps the right people in the right places. A project that you're working on today can be terminated tomorrow through no fault of your own. Your workplace is a microcosm of the external marketplace. Yesterday's success is a weak predictor of tomorrow's outcomes. Competition between Olympic athletes can remind us of this truth.

On the management end, it's not enough to reward 10 percent of your workforce in the hopes that they will stay put, make things productive, or guarantee success. Workers at all levels must develop a "self-led worklife." This means taking responsibility and joining in. You join, for example, when you ask for meetings with your boss instead of waiting to be summoned. You also join when you decide on a training program or course that would benefit your career mobility and your company's productivity and discuss that program's relevancy with your boss and then ask her to consider it as a budget item. And, you join when you ask a prospective employer to provide you with their customers' names so that you can talk with them before you make a decision about accepting a new job. One outcome of worklife self-leadership is mobility—the ability to see and seek alternatives and make choices that benefit you, the worker, and your organization, or customer.

Working "With"
for Mobility and Productivity

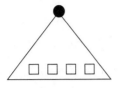

Working "For"	**Working "With"**
A Dependent	An Independent and Interdependent,
Hierarchical Model	Peer-Work Model

The triangle above illustrates a working for others hierarchy. The circle at the top represents the boss. Workers are depicted by the four squares, and roles are tightly defined, inhibiting the flow of ideas and spontaneous, customer-focused action. The worker gives but doesn't equally receive, jeopardizing healthy moral and sustained productivity. In contrast, the seven-circle honeycomb to the right demonstrates a working with configuration. Each circle denotes a worker who has chosen inter-dependence—to work with others to solve problems and innovate. The worker experiences a give and take system. One circle has a darker border, signifying independence—self-direction and self-expression—as you come together to join your peers. Peers, in this archetype, support you to materialize individual and organizational goals as every player is feed by personal commitment to succeed and contribute.

Compare these models to your current work situation. How could you increase your mobility and productivity by more consciously working with others? The following section offers some suggestions.

Work is Personal

As you increase your ability to join, work becomes more personal and you deepen your belief that "I am independent and interdependent. I am determined to join these two parts of me, releasing me further from the shackles of dependence." As a result, you increase your self-confidence, charter new territory, and attract opportunity. Below is a "personal" list of attributes that have come from my clients as they work with, not for, others.

You can...

- Embrace work as a matter of your soul.
- Listen to your gut.
- Think before you give up your time.
- View ambiguity as part of change and growth.
- Give yourself permission to explore.
- See the world as a school without walls.
- Respect others and yourself for trying.
- Learn joyfully as you problem solve irreverently.
- Replace anxiety with asking your questions.
- Hold on to what works for you.
- Go for your dream no matter what others think.
- Let go of what does not work.
- Insist on combining your skill and passion.
- Hope precisely.
- Self-lead every day of your life.
- Collaborate and contribute to make things better
- Quit, to do the right thing.

Be true to thine ownself.

—*William Shakespeare*

Peer Work—Worklife Development Review

Peer work—a design for individual and team development and productivity—involves a worklife development review, at least once a year, for workers at all levels. I use the term "worklife," not only "work" and or "career," as highlighted in the introduction, because as you mature healthy work decisions can only be made when you consider and integrate other aspects of life. This review would be initiated by the organization and it would be the responsibility of all workers to arrange a meeting with their boss to discuss their past development activities and future development plans.

All workers would be prepared to...

- ≣ briefly summarize the development activities (training, special programs, counseling) that they have been involved in over the past 12 months.
- ≣ discuss the contributions they have made to their department, customers, organization over the previous 12 months.
- ≣ comment on how any extracurricular activities have influenced their worklife and performance over the previous 12 months.
- ≣ identify the types of activities and responsibilities they would like to have more of in their current and future work.
- ≣ list and discuss personal qualities and job skills they would like to work on during the upcoming twelve months to improve their present job performance and achieve their personal career goals.

The organization would join the workers by...

- ≣ creating "compensation bands" or flexible reward systems that support job development and movement—the lattice— commensurate with individual needs and organizational goals.
- ≣ respecting all individuals for their courage to initiate, participate, grow, and change and by honoring the confidentiality of personal information.

- ≣ providing worklife development resources (books, inventories, special programs, learning forums, Web assistance, and counsel) for individuals.
- ≣ posting internal job opportunities and encouraging workers to interview for those positions.
- ≣ staying open and flexible to worker transition as a necessary part of the development and productivity process.

For career planning purposes you and your organization can use the tool on the following page. Share it with your boss and other workers. Use it during your worklife development review or at any stage of your process as a guide for optimizing your career success and productivity. If you are between jobs or looking for your first job, follow this plan or adapt it in ways that serve your purposes.

Worklife Action Plan

Self-Leadership and Management

Name: _____**Date:**_____

This plan will help you to clarify your goal and identify the methods and steps necessary to achieve it. Either on your own or with a colleague, first write down one goal (A) that you'd like to achieve (e.g., close a sale, run a collaborative meeting, learn a new accounting procedure). Second, clarify the benefits to you and your customer (B and C). Third, decide what tools and resources (D) you'll need to achieve this goal (e.g., people, coaching, training, money). Fourth, articulate the process or steps for getting there (E). This plan, as with other successful working plans, is meant to be flexible; you'll make changes as you proceed.

A. My goal or objective is to clarify what I want do next toward finding another position within my company.

B. The benefits to me will be utilizing my strengths, refocused energy, and feeling happier about not only how I feel in my work, but also at home.

C. The benefits to my company and customers will be increased productivity and commitment to customer needs.

D. The tools and resources I'll need to fulfill this objective are as follows:

≣ Skills inventory	≣ Worklife counseling sessions
≣ Networking with colleagues	≣ Values inventory
≣ Discussions with boss	≣ Reading relevant articles and books

E. These are the steps I'll take, although they may change as I proceed:

1. Meet with worklife counselor   **When** Tuesday, April 8, 20__

2. Take inventories   **When** Wednesday, April 16, 20__

3. Discuss plans with boss   **When** Friday, April 18, 20__

4. Network for options   **When** One interview a week for one month

5. Continue worklife counsel   **When** One session a week for one month. Read relevant information between sessions.

6. Update my spouse about concerns and progress   **When** During breakfast on Saturdays

When You Work With, Know Your Customers

You can also treat your customers as your equals. A customer is an individual or an organization who benefits from your interaction with them. Every stage of production or service involves a customer. The person sitting next to you is your customer; you get paid—indirectly or directly—to serve him or her. Who is sitting next to you—a manager? A salesperson? An assembler? A programmer? A secretary? A stockholder? A fellow musician? An employer? Your customer may be depending on you for up-to-date stock information, a final draft of a report, the harmony while you play the melody, or a satisfactory assembly-line inspection.

People working at all levels inside organizations, even the president, have customers. The president must satisfy the stockholders and ultimately answer to the buyer. If enough buyers are dissatisfied, the president will be held accountable and may lose customers and, possibly, his or her job. The sales manager also has customers, both the sales staff and you, the buyers of the product or service. And the administrative assistant has one or more customers, including a manager and other staff who need backup support. In each case, the continuity of the customer-worker relationship depends on the recognition and satisfaction of customers' needs. If a high-tech company manufactures small-screen computers and the customer wants one with a large screen, the company needs to adapt or the customer will buy elsewhere. And if the manager promised the salesperson to deliver a large-screen computer in one week and there is a delay, the manager must then deal with the disgruntled customer.

Merchants, these days, know that customers only pay for satisfying service. In an area town center, there are two famous coffee retailers located just 25 yards from each other. I entered one to buy a quick cup of coffee, and was ignored. Before the server could say a word, I took my business next door. When I'm in that town next, I'll go first to where I was served. Competition keeps any viable merchant committed to their goal: serving the customer.

Peer Work Requires Relevancy

The days are over of just making something, packaging it, and expecting others to buy it. Frederick, the editor of an executive newsletter, gets paid for delivering timely, practical advice to his professional readership. He also gets paid to ask his readers about their ideas and interests and to communicate those ideas and interests to other journalists. In addition, he frequently asks his staff about their ideas and insights. In a nutshell, he gathers and synthesizes information and manages and consults with his staff in an effort to deliver succinct and worthwhile information. He will continue to get paid if the newsletter meets the needs of his readership. Frederick commented, "My work must be germane to my readership. The readers must be benefiting from my actions or I wouldn't get paid. I could possibly lose my job; worst case, this publication could go down the tubes."

We can see ourselves as workers who accept and do the same old repetitive work or as contributors who add to the profitability of the company by delivering a valued service to the customer. But, it is not enough simply to *do* or to *sell* your product or service. You must first conduct research to determine if your proposal or service will satisfy the customer. In Maya's case, for example, she manages a group of salespeople and was planning to present a program to them on how to close a sale. She first asked the staff members—her peers—what *they* wanted to learn. They said they would benefit more from a program on how to listen. Therefore, Maya's first plan would have been irrelevant, so she reassessed the relevancy of her first proposal and redesigned her training seminar accordingly.

For job seekers, the art of peer work—matching skill with customer—is essential. The prospective customer or employer will undoubtedly wonder, "How can this person I am interviewing solve my problems?" Be prepared to give examples of what you do that can be useful to your customer or potential employer. A "self-employed" attitude requires worklife leadership, the ongoing examination of your skills and values and the practice of using them to address the needs of different customers.

Howard had been managing the family carpet business and then decided to pursue his studies in health care management. He invested time and money to develop his skills. Howard's general goal was to find work that would utilize his education and interests. He was upset because he wasn't sure that school was meeting his career needs. It was, however, a place where he could hang his hat on a daily basis. It kept him busy and focused but ultimately out of touch with the world of work.

As we explored his concerns, Howard identified a gap in his career development process. He was accepted into the program but had not talked with people in the health care management field about how they had applied their education and experience to their current situation. Howard concluded that he needed to network so he could better understand how his previous work experience could be combined with his education to establish a specific career goal. School is not an "answer" but it can be a valuable tool and credential, especially as you clarify what you bring to the marketplace and how you can apply your unique skills and talents.

You Can Meet Your Needs and Your Customers' Needs

Whether you are employed full- or part-time, changing careers, laid off and looking for the same type of work, or a recent college graduate, your success is contingent upon matching your skills, values, and interests with customers' needs. You can only create a job, retain your current job, or find a new job if you add value to customers—and in this way, serve your peers.

Think about the following questions, and answer them to the best of your ability. Feel free to discuss your thoughts and answers with a colleague.

1. What do you specifically do to meet the needs of your customers or potential employer?

   Example: I ask a question before I offer a solution.

2. How do you know when your customers, employer, or the person with whom you are interviewing is satisfied?

   Example: I know my customers are satisfied when they request a repeat order as a result of my thorough and accurate research regarding their concerns about the product.

Identify Your Customers

I could not answer this question any better than by quoting Marsha Selva. She states, "My customers are my profit. I am overhead, they are profit."

To identify your customers, try answering the following questions. Before you answer, think about who your customers are and what you specifically do to provide service.

1. How do you define your customers?

   Example: Most of my customers are midlife professionals seeking renewal. They are working inside and outside of companies, and are now questioning their happiness, focus, or lack of meaningful direction. As well, my customers may be between jobs. Most want to examine and clarify their strengths and learn how to articulate them clearly with passion. They are searching for what they really want in worklife and how to materialize new goals as they combine joy and productivity. In addition, my customers are managers and executives inside of organizations concerned with learning how to do their jobs better.

2. What are some of your customers' needs?

Example: My customers need to talk about their worklife experiences and sort out and make decisions about what skills they want to use and improve what values they want to honor in the next stage of their worklife.

Face Your Customers

Add value. That's your basic goal. Workers are evaluated by their customers, not merely by faceless organizations. Every worker—president, vice president, manager, and staff—reports to the customer. So, when you propose an idea to a group, present a business plan to a banker, or interview for a job, *their* questions is, "How will you benefit the customer?"

If you've done your inner work—assessed who you are and what you want—your next step is to harness your resources in such a way that they'll add value to the customer. Lisa, the scriptwriter, did this when she answered the question, "What will others buy from me?" Helen, a former lawyer, found that she was a historian at heart. She combined her love for the classics, her law background, and her ability to write by first clarifying and prioritizing her own needs and then identifying a consulting firm. In her new role, she researches and writes histories of corporations. She has created a niche that has meaning for her *and* attracts *and* serves the customer.

It won't work for job seekers, career changers, workers within organizations, or consultants to simply solicit jobs. To reach your goal successfully you must share your passion and ideas, and demonstrate how you can serve the customer. Tim, senior vice president of human resources with a *Fortune 500* company said, "It's a huge mistake to focus on yourself exclusively. I meet too many people who fail to ask questions...recognize and understand the company's needs. I want to know how he or she will use their skills to benefit us. This is the information I need to communicate to the hiring managers, my customers." Organizations can't afford to hire the wrong person, and customers are the key rule makers: "Provide quality services and products at a fair price or I'll go elsewhere."

Have you done your research? If not, it's nearly impossible to know how you'll add value. Start by looking for a job that you'd *like* or by analyzing a problem in or outside of your company which you would like to work on. Ask a librarian for research assistance and read everything that you can get your hands on about the organization: its place in the market sector, the outside forces that influence its business, and what makes people successful in your chosen professional area. If you are researching a company, for example, go to your favorite search engine to find out who the customers are, what products and/or services they have bought, who the competition is, and what the organizational culture is like.

In your search, if you always keep in mind that *your* job is to match your abilities and interests with the needs of the customer, then you will achieve your goal: to find a meaningful job, start a business, create a niche, or lead a company.

I'm my own employer. CRM [the company] is my customer.

—*Kirby Timmons*

Ten Commandments for Winning Interviews

The Ten Commandments for Winning Interviews were first published in my book, *When You Lose Your Job* (Berrett-Koehler, 1992). They subsequently appeared in the *National Business Employment Weekly* and won the Ten Best Article Award for 1993 from the *National Business Employment Weekly*. The commandments are biblical yet profoundly relevant today, whether you work inside or outside of an organization. I've tweaked them here and there as a means for you to work with, not for, your organization and customers.

Know your past achievements. An achievement is something that you enjoyed doing, that excited you, and that gave you a feeling of pride. Achievements might include selling your paintings, developing a new product, or designing and delivering a presentation. Each achievement is made up of several factors: creativity, management, directing, leading, selling, or tenacity. Your core skills may be found by writing stories about your successes. Then, by underlining the qualities you used most frequently, your core skills will emerge.

Do your research. Gather and analyze information about the company and its competition. Your painstaking research includes finding out what the company produces, who its customers are, what its culture is like, its mission. Also, find out if the company has restructured in the past year, if it is growing and why, what its most recent annual revenues were, its priorities and primary competition, how many workers are employed, and who the company's primary competition is. If you are interviewing for a specific position, try to get some information about the organization and where this position fits into the structure, who it reports to, and what that person's title is. Your knowledge about them will not only contribute to your self-confidence, but also show them that you are sincere.

Answer all questions directly. Don't get long-winded or go off on unrelated tangents. *The best insurance for a direct response is to listen, do your company research, and to know your skills, achievements, values and personal qualities.* Listening and preparation are the keys to peer work at an interview. Decision makers, like you, are busy; they don't have time to listen to you ramble. This is an opportunity for you to demonstrate your effective, practical, and solution-oriented work style.

Be prepared to answer personal questions. Your personality and core values are strongly considered in a competitive market. Every person counts. You will not only contribute to the profitability of the company but also to its culture. You may be asked, "What are you passionate about? What are your shortcomings? What is it about yourself that you'd like to change? What do you want to contribute most to this organization? What is your top value? Describe your best or worst boss in your career history?" (Remember, never berate or bad mouth a former boss. Always put a positive, constructive spin on how you discuss this issue.)

Balance listening and questioning with telling your story. Do not interrupt or sit back (don't slouch or try to act cool) when your interviewer is talking. Ask a few good questions, including "What are the company's priorities? Regarding this position, what would you like a new person to step in and do first?" Be brief when telling a story or answering a question. Pause from time to time and ask questions such as, "Would you like me to continue? Am I answering your question? Is there any aspect of my background that is of most interest?"

Focus on what you can do for them. The employer is interested in how you can solve their problems and work with their customers. The employer wants an excellent match but does not want to think about how this position will provide you with an opportunity to apply your skills and experience. Do not operate out of a "job description mentality" that emphasizes title, position, and narrowly defined responsibilities. Today, businesses are focusing on the customer. They look for people whose primary concern is the customer and the company, those who want to roll up their sleeves, get to work, and be a team player.

Let the company raise the issue of compensation. Remember this golden rule: If you bring up money first, you lose. All companies want to hire the best person for the job, especially in a competitive marketplace. They'll make you an offer if you've done your homework and shown them the relevancy of your experience and ability to meet their needs. If you are asked, "What would you like?" Respond, "I'd like you to make me an offer." Then you'll have additional information from which to think over their proposal, prepare a counter offer, and negotiate.

Be bold—state your interest and why. In a competitive business market companies want people who know what they want and why. Interviewers are often not prepared. So, do your personal and company research. If the company and the specific job interest you, say so and why. For example, the organization may have similar values to yours regarding professional growth and development or their product or service could contribute to the environment in a way in which you approve of. At the end of the interview be sure to express your interest: ask what you can expect next, how many candidates are being considered, and when a decision is expected to be made.

Relate your past experience to their needs. Hearsay is that all companies are looking for workers with experience in their specific industry. Baloney! *Be prepared to demonstrate how your experience and skills are allied with their needs.* For example, tell a story about how you consistently met customers' needs and give examples of your fair and productive management style. Excellence in customer service and management are highly transferable if you can clearly demonstrate how. You can also give specific examples of how your involvement resulted in significant revenue growth; for example, I was responsible for a revenue growth of 50% (from $2mm to $4mm) when I managed the retail division.

Expand your options. Set up as many interviews as possible, even when you think you have a hot prospect. You don't have the job until you've signed the acceptance letter. The job market is unpredictable—a company that you're sure is going to make you an offer could loose a contract or an internal candidate could emerge to adversely effect your candidacy. Also, you will be a much stronger negotiator if you know the market and have other active possibilities.

Actively Working With Others

As the Ten Commandments for Winning Interviews suggest, current times call for a different mindset: *actively working with others*, a process in which you, the individual, the learning-to-be-self-employed contributor, are asking questions, sharing ideas, and putting energy into solving problems and serving your customer, colleague, and organization. Simply stated, achieving your goals involves active alliances—peer relationships—within the constantly changing, flatter, more competitive workplace. The organization requires your initiative and input when hierarchical barriers become more flexible or are removed. I've heard countless bosses say, "I want people to come forward with what they want to do. Very few workers take the initiative. They play it safe."

The *concept* of actively working with others isn't new. For most of you, its newness will probably be in the *practice*. The ongoing advancements in aviation, computers, and agriculture, for example, grew out of the active joining of resources between government and private enterprise. Each member learned to be open to the other's ideas, thereby creating the inspiration and resources for better products and services. In the area of renewal, my clients are constantly sharing feedback as generated through their insights, efforts to explore, and successes. Dawn mentioned, "It's so valuable to me that you are able to synthesize my thoughts and prioritize next steps. I like that, before a session ends, you always suggest one or two concrete things to do next. I may add to your suggestions or tweak what you say but bottom line, for me, this focusing method works." Because many of my clients have given me similar feedback, I vigilantly hunt for and assign the most relevant steps that each client would most benefit from between sessions.

Sam commented, "Exploring the marketplace when I'm not sure about my direction is the toughest part of transition for me. Your ideas and insights, supportive reminder [to] 'go for it!' and my field research give me the courage to put my ego aside, knock on another door, and ask a person I've never met to listen to my story and ask them about theirs." A feeling of being less than or losing what one was in the past haunts and halts many people in transition. Sam was a business partner in a printing business that no longer exists due to technical advancements. Now one computer performs specialized printing processes cheaper, more efficiently, and better then Sam's former team. He must take his old I'm-the-boss hat off and replace it with a new I'm-the-boss attitude. Actively working with others makes Sam's journey—letting go and moving on—more possible.

Actively working with others is the process of creating a bridge between what you believe, do, and contribute and your organization's, customer's, or client's needs. The beauty of actively working with others is in the way that people take the initiative and participate in developing creative answers to problems in the workplace. For instance, Carlos, a hospital administrator, thought, "How can I develop and sell new programs to community groups?" Developing and selling the programs, he discovered, would probably work best through actively joining the groups. Carlos gave himself permission to experiment.

To begin, he made a list of the community groups that he thought would benefit most from preventive health care programs. Next, he clearly defined and wrote down his proposed ideas and read them aloud to a colleague. Carlos then called each client and said something like, "I'd like to develop some new preventive health care services that will better serve your group. Your input is vital. Would you and a small group from your organization be willing to meet with me? The purpose of the meeting is for our organization to learn about some of your needs and ideas and to share some of ours. I plan to meet with five other community groups. I'd be happy to review my collective findings with you in exchange for your time and insights."

In effect, Carlos created a bridge between community groups (one customer) and his organization (another customer). He took the initiative to develop and expand services for his primary customer, the hospital. He asked what his community customers needed and shared those needs with his colleagues, eventually developing tailored programs of mutual benefit.

Mobilizing Workers: Retaining Them Won't Work

In discussions with organizational clients I often hear, "Our problem is that we have to figure out a strategy for retaining employees. We've downsized and can't afford to lose any more employees. Can you write a proposal outlining how to do this?" My answer is, "I could, but I have no interest." Retaining workers (my term!) doesn't make sense in a mobile world. Flexibility, knowledge, challenge, and clarity do.

Instead, I recommend that the organization create a program focused on worklife self-leadership and management for workers at all levels. This program will provide support and tools for all workers to know themselves better and to make personal and professional decisions and contributions. Companies need to earn the devotion, loyalty, and energy of their workers so that they feel freer to join.

The word "retain" means to keep one's position or to hold in one place. An image comes to mind of a retaining wall, a structure designed to keep at bay a formidable force. Retaining devices and systems do not guarantee organizational stability and productivity; they create a false reality. We need to encourage working with others—peer work—a design for individual and team development and productivity. Retaining inhibits receiving, an essential element of peer work.

Retaining is Impersonal, Receiving is Personal

Chopping ice can be dangerous; chips of ice fly around, but mostly the job is just tiring. You don't get very far very fast. Before you've made much progress, your joints usually ache and sometimes your head smarts. Wisdom tells us to spread sand as a precaution and wait as the sun melts the ice. Seth, a broadcast director said, "I'm sick of chopping ice. I want to take advantage of the sunshine." Sometimes, however, chopping ice is necessary to shake up your current beliefs.

"I think the thing that has helped me most in being open to receiving," said Patsy, another client, "is to allow my natural friendliness and curiosity to come out with other people. When I think about it, most of my important 'breakthroughs' have begun when I initiated a conversation with a stranger or someone I didn't know well. It was usually just a casual thing—certainly not goal driven. It's amazing what people will tell you if you show genuine interest and ask questions.

"During a very difficult period in my corporate career, I started dreaming of a job where I could get away from the rat race and back to nature. Perhaps I'd house-sit someone's vacation ranch property out West and start writing in my free time. I carried this idea around with me for three years, thinking I had dreamed it up. Two months ago, I started up a conversation with a fellow shopper and landlord while waiting in line at the grocery store. I asked him how turnover was going with his tenants and he told me that one had left recently to manage a ranch out West. My jaw fell open, but I collected it enough to ask for the woman's name and phone number. The call to this woman revealed that my dream was a well-established profession, replete with recruitment agencies and [a] trade publication."

Oftentimes, you have to break up the old in order to receive the new.

Organizational Commitment to Worker Satisfaction

Kyle, a vice president of research and development at a large computer manufacturer, is embarking on a mission to "increase employee satisfaction" in his division. "We have no choice," he said "but to increase worker morale if we want to survive and compete." The research and development team has been working toward the goal of reducing the product development cycle time from two to three years to eight to nine months. Achieving and sustaining this goal takes continued commitment, diligence, and expertise. As a result, the expert senior workers are getting pressured to perform, thus leaving little opportunity for the less advanced workers, or so-called junior workers, to advance or participate. Since the goal has been to reduce cycle time and manufacture quality products, the company can't afford to spend time and money on training workers.

From a career perspective, the senior workers are at the top of the ladder, doing the work, running the show, and feeling confined in a "performance box." The message to them is simply "Do your job. Stick it out." They have a position and a paycheck. Junior workers, on the other hand, are blocked in their careers. They have been discouraged from experimenting and learning, and they no longer have a ladder to climb. They are thinking, "If I can't move up, I'll move out." Some have, in fact, left the company. This organization, like most competitive organizations, cannot afford to lose budding talent.

The workers at this firm have increased productivity, and their compensation levels are competitive. Yet, to the company's chagrin and despite a difficult job market, talented workers are still leaving. Job motivation and satisfaction cannot be guaranteed by offering higher salaries and promotions. Such resources have been strip mined. It is the responsibility of all workers to pay more attention to the less tangible, more elusive factors that add up to worker satisfaction.

Many of my clients are "making a good income" yet are hungry to feel more connected to their work. They want to live in the moment—not for a paycheck or the weekend. Abigale said, "I would like to pursue something different—my corporate executive hat no longer fits. I want to tap into areas that I have not yet cultivated but are really naturals for me. The first is an artistic way of looking at things—whatever that means or gets translated into—and the second is work that may be more hands-on rather than analytical."

Some have been laid off and have made it their worklife goal to combine joy and productivity. Jean, former director of a nonprofit organization, said, "Right at the moment, I feel like I'm sitting in the middle of the Pacific Ocean and I've been asked, 'Where do you want to go?' I say, 'A place where I can have fun, be challenged, and provide leadership.'

I guess I'm struggling with choosing a country. It needs to be one that shares my values or I won't be happy or productive." Others continue to work as a means to fuel their bliss, providing the resources to buy time—to ask questions and search for answers—that will lead them to their heart's desire and connect them to meaningful work. Blake, a management consultant, said, "I want to be able to relax more and feel less afraid. I don't want to have a pit in my stomach when I wake up to go to work."

These people have learned that competitive salary levels rarely are enough to keep workers. Eventually they will leave to seek a workplace that offers personal satisfaction, recognition from others, and a good income.

A study done by Kyle's task force showed that one of the primary reasons for "worker dissatisfaction" was the "lack of career options and development." As a result, the organization embarked upon a career *self*-leadership and management program. Its three primary objectives were as follows:

1. To educate staff in worklife self-leadership and management to help empower all staff members to take responsibility for their worklife mobility and job productivity.

2. To guide staff in the use of specific worklife tools for the purpose of enhancing self-confidence and developing a deeper partnership between individual needs and organization goals.

3. To coach and support staff to take specific worklife initiatives that will result in increased worklife satisfaction and job productivity.

This program was introduced as a learning partnership between the company and the staff for *optimizing* individual worklife success and job productivity. It was not a placement or outplacement program.

Handling the Transition

Suspending judgment and adopting curiosity—questioning, researching, exploring—takes courage. Johanna, an anthropologist and professor, remarked, "My associates know I'm making a career change and they keep asking, 'What are you doing?' 'What are you going to do?' They are uncomfortable with my answer; it is vague. I'm not ready to judge or put closure on my process. For once in my life I need to sit back, observe the world and myself. To charge forward as if I'm going for another PhD at this point would be counterproductive. Instead, it's like I'm on an archaeological dig. I'm exploring. Who knows what I'll find?"

Johanna's curiosity, which is not linked to a specific goal, goes against many people's values and experience. Johanna's colleagues were uncomfortable with the degree of uncertainty in her life. Such people want answers: "I earn $50,000" or "I'm a forest ecologist" or "I'm a vice president with a start-up nonprofit organization" or "I'm laid off" or "I've been interviewing, and finally, I'm one of two candidates for a job." If you must give an answer, say, "I'm exploring. Do you mind if I ask you a question?" A "self-employed" attitude requires curiosity—a means to extend your personal and professional boundaries and update your career or business choices. Note the difference between the curious and judging statements in the following examples. If you think of more comparative statements, write them down.

> Curious: I wonder why zebras have stripes?
> Judging: I don't like zebra stripes.
>
> Curious: I wonder what makes those people successful?
> Judging: They were probably born with a silver spoon in their mouth.

Curious: During my interview next week I'm going to ask about the top priorities currently driving the company.

Judging: This company is like all the rest, they just want people to put their heads down, produce, and ask few questions.

Find a Mentor

Early in my business career, I had a boss and mentor, Irv Sands. Irv believed in me when I wasn't quite sure what I believed. I mentioned that Irv was my boss because it's important for people to have someone that they respect and look up to. Irv offered me his experience and the guidance that I craved. He knew I had the basic skill and aptitude to do the job and was intrigued by the ways that I experimented, took risks, and eventually succeeded. Irv was curious at first. This boss/mentor influence was the most significant catalyst in my business career. Irv encouraged my questions and the gestation of my belief that I could run a profitable business using my integrity, a core part of my spirit and power. He listened to me ask clients, "What do you really want to do?" He supported my process of listening, probing, and supporting them as they explored to arrive at their answer. I passed on the development of my curiosity to my clients.

Irv maintained an open-door policy and would often invite me for coffee to discuss what I was learning and how I might overcome any obstacles that I encountered. When I asked a question, Irv would respond, "What do *you* think?" Irv often reminded me that he respected my expertise, opinions, and unique style; they were refreshing and valuable to the firm and its clientele. Basically, he fostered a working "with," independent and interdependent, relationship. I never forgot that he was the boss, though I felt that I was the boss, too.

If we all had an Irv, someone who was a boss and mentor, at some point in our lives, we would undoubtedly progress beyond our expectations and in return support others. Mentoring does not have to be restricted to a relationship with only one other person. People can carefully choose to join *teams* and *organizations* and find that the community or group can be a mentor. These teams and organizations provide support, direction, and opportunities for growth and contribution. They possess values, mission statements, stimulating projects, and rewards.

According to Rene Petrin, president of Management Mentors, "Mentoring has the power to transform both mentors and mentorees. Both have something to give one another, and it is in this sharing that each can grow in separate ways and become givers and receivers. Mentors will often report that they feel they've gotten as much, if not more, from the relationship. We understand how mentorees benefit, but mentors, too, can appreciate how much they have, by sharing what they have. They can also feel renewed enthusiasm for their own career by seeing what they have offered others and they can bring ideas shared by the mentoree to their own work or workplace, thus influencing their own success as well."

Clarify Your Values

Coming to terms with your value system is essential when collaborating with a team. It's also part of the necessary inner work for developing a self-employed attitude. Your values are not set in stone. If they were, change would be impossible. The inner work helps you to recognize your present values, thus enhancing your self-esteem and spurring you to action.

As you clarify and prioritize your values, you will make positive choices. Valerie, when exploring a transition from the corporation to consulting, made it a point in her discussions with colleagues to say, "It's a priority that I work with a management consulting firm that is socially conscious. It's not enough just to increase profits." As she networked and interviewed, she was guided by this value and listened for information that would help her make an educated choice.

Doing your inner work fuels your outer mobility, too. Without your inner work you would not be able to share what you believe or to apply your own personal standards to make critical decisions. If one of your values is "doing work that benefits people," then you won't pursue work that doesn't meet that criterion. Sometimes, naturally, you will be enticed by other possibilities (e.g., money, travel, leading others, a title). When your core values are compromised, however, you may well end up with a job or new project but will eventually be unhappy with your choice.

Gail, a school superintendent, said, "My passion can be viewed as the intersection of philosophy, psychology, and business. Philosophically, I believe in doing work that makes people's lives better. Psychology comes into play in understanding why people do what they do. Business involves influencing them. I am at my best when I use all three in my work." Gail makes difficult choices. She looks at the facts before she makes a decision; there is too much at stake otherwise. But she uses her passion to help her make decisions. Determination, using "will" alone, can lead to drudgery and frustration after a protracted period of time.

Whatever you discover about yourself, your inner work will *never* be wasted. It gives life and shape to your vision, whatever the outcome. I want you to hear and embrace those words. As you and the world continue to change, the inner work is your only real security. The fruits of this work are in experiencing the commitment and energy to express and realize your goals and to serve others.

An In and an Out

The concept of working with others emphasizes flexibility, not complacency or rigidity. By this time you know the maxim, "You must know and be loyal to yourself." The contract, or employer and employee dependence, has been rewritten. In the new terms, every worker needs an "in" and an "out" as a means to ensure their success and survival. Commit fully to a three-month project but be prepared to renegotiate your situation or leave if the joining process has not been mutually beneficial. David, a former architect, opened a fast-food franchise. He bought in and also developed an alternative plan (out) in the event that running the franchise didn't meet his expectations. David later decided to sell the franchise because the 80-hour-a-week schedule required for running a successful operation did not allow enough time for other obligations in his life. The franchiser bought the business back. Sally, a senior technician, was laid off by one division in her company; soon after, she was offered a position in another division. Although relieved by the offer, Sally made a six-month commitment to herself in which she would do her work (in) and prepare for leaving (out) if her arrangement was unsatisfying. Give yourself both an "in" and an "out." Develop a financial cushion and know your strengths—skills, passion, purpose, values—and the marketplace.

Peer work is creating work from which both parties benefit.
Peer work...

without obligation and
with purpose.

without fear and
with passion and purpose.

without dependence and
with independence and interdependence.

without signed contracts and
with personal commitment.

without drudgery and
with authenticity, collaboration, and productivity.

Who's the Boss?
Check-In: Working With, Not For, Your Organization and Customers

1. What do you recall as your most enjoyable and productive times at work?

2. Can you remember a situation at work when you collaborated (worked with) a colleague or boss? What happened? How might you replicate this behavior now? Can you recall a time at work when you felt subordinated (worked for) a colleague or boss? What happened? How might you change your behavior to alter this situation should it arise again?

3. When have you drawn a line in the sand at work? When have you walked away from a situation because your values were compromised?

4. Who are your customers? What are some of their needs? How do you work with them to fulfill their needs? How do you think you best serve your customer? How might you improve your working relationship? Might you adjust your attitude from working "for" to working "with"?

5. Is it time for you to talk with your boss about what else you'd like to do and how you might benefit the company? What do you want to say to him or her? Write it down and rehearse what you have to say with a friend or colleague. Keep the question in mind, "How might I approach my boss as a peer?"

COMMITTING TO
CONTINUOUS LEARNING

View your worklife as an ongoing journey

EMPLOYED ATTITUDE
Dependent Mindset

I can hold on to my successes and be satisfied. If I can only get what I want—position, title, benefits—I can rest on my past accomplishments.

SELF-EMPLOYED ATTITUDE
Independent and Interdependent Mindset

I will commit to my continuous curiosity, personal growth, and gaining new perspectives. My worklife is an ongoing journey. My mistakes and successes lead to expanded thinking and further contribution.

Chapters 6 and 7, Committing to Continuous Learning and Creating a Meaningful Worklife, are essential for navigating a changed work world because you are an evolving human being and the world is, at its core, a state of constant churn and flux. Without continuous learning and creating meaningful work, how would we find a cure for cancer, enjoy new forms of art and music, imagine and act on peaceful alternatives, generate renewable resources, and restore ourselves?

**I like a state of continued becoming, with a goal
in front and not behind.**

—George Bernard Shaw

Lucinda, a single mother and a high-tech sales person, has been "pushing to survive" all her life. She's raised a healthy, vibrant son and has earned enough money to pay the bills—and then some. Now it's time to attend to learning more about what she wants, and how to create what *she* wants in her worklife. Thriving, for Lucinda, does not equate to earning more money. She said, "How many more pairs of shoes do I need?" In transition and feeling anxious, Lucinda forgets (as do many), deferring to her fear, about her ability to learn and create.

She said, "What if I fail when I explore new areas of work?" I reminded Lucinda, "We'll figure out incremental steps to minimize your risk. In today's world it's even riskier not to re-create yourself. Yesterday's jobs are becoming extinct...look at all those high-tech positions that disappeared with the dot-com bust. Besides, your wheels are in motion: you've been talking with me because you want to grow personally and contribute in new ways. Now you're getting ready to learn from others and test your ideas in the world. All your life you've survived and might I add thrived. With your experience as a mom and a salesperson, you've honed some finely tuned learning-and-creating muscles. Your current job is to remember that you have these strengths and to put your muscles to work."

Lucinda responded, "Thinking about what you've said, and about my roles as mom and business woman, I have learned to listen, nurture ideas and others, develop relationships, manage projects, communicate with and influence all kinds of people, and figure out how to close impossible deals. If I let myself think positively, these are the strengths I can parlay into my future."

I believe in the power of words. Over 20 years ago, I encountered Scott Peck's notion that "life is difficult." These three words transformed my life. During the same time period, David, a colleague and customer, sent me a note that said, "This world needs you," a thought that had never occurred to me. Since then I've been inspired to help others like Lucinda by passing on this message through writing, counseling, and speaking.

"This world needs *you*," can be part of your interdependence. As you deepen your independence—trade fears for hopes—it behooves you to foster your interdependence—connecting with and contributing more to the world.

Frank Ostaseski, founding director of The Zen Hospice Project, said, "The nature of fear is that it separates us from the people around us, from ourselves. When we can come into contact with this fear without running in the other direction, we can make some peace with it." Frank trains a 100-member volunteer staff to form deep bonds with patients.

Below are two lists of words. In the left column you will see a list of fear words that block continuous learning. Individually, each represents a huge rock placed in front of every step you take, inhibiting your imagination and hindering your movement toward possibility and opportunity. Combined, they form a retaining wall that barricades your exploration and growth and obstructs your self-expression and contribution.

Fear Words	*Freedom Words*
Stagnation	*Continuous Learning*
Anxiety	Curiosity
Worry	Hope
Rigidity	Flexibility
Hiding	Seeking

Before I understood that life was difficult and that the world needed me I felt blocked by anxiety, worry, and rigidity. For many years now, I've traded in the fear words in the left column for *freedom* words in the right column. These words—curiosity, hope, and flexibility—are catalysts. You can actively utilize them to enhance your personal worklife. Curiosity fed my journey to speak about a self-employed attitude in Haiti. Had I capitulated to my anxiety, I never would have had this adventure.

You, too, can trade fear for freedom. Your conscious attention to the words in the right column can shift your perspective from an employed to a self-employed attitude and serve you in the moment and during your lifetime. For my client Patricia, who wanted to change from work in the nonprofit sector to a position in a corporation, using written words to express her dilemma freed her and enabled her to confront her fears. As part of her transition process, Patricia often e-mailed her thoughts to me:

> My father believed that when suffering and pain come our way, we should get on our knees in gratefulness, for amazing blessings and opportunity are born in these moments. Though I remain mindful of these words, and cling to the wonderment that such moments brought me throughout my life, presently I... feel so very overwhelmed by the uncertainty. I want to feel excited about the endless possibilities that exist in uncertainty, but sometimes I feel as though I am losing my way.

The ongoing process of journal writing, having a private place to record her thoughts and share them as she wishes, has helped Patricia. Like a good friend, her journal provides an opportunity to express her feelings and brainstorm without judgment. As she rereads her thoughts, Patricia learns when she is fed by anxiety versus curiosity and when she is fueled by worry versus hope. With her feelings and behaviors before her, she can more easily identify and let go of the unproductive ones. When we met we talked about her fears, which included judging by others and wasting precious time as she feels stuck. Patricia left with a specific assignment that gave her structure and moved her closer to her dream. It was to look up the alumni list from her graduating class and pinpoint five or six women she thought were doing interesting work. Next she was to prepare three or four exploratory questions that she could ask each. For example, "How did you choose your current work?" "What do you specifically like about it?" "If you could change one thing about your work, what would it be?" Developing these questions helped Patricia organize her thoughts and increased her confidence. She agreed to limit the number of questions she would ask to allow time for free expression. Then she contacted each person on her list for exploring, not job searching, purposes.

Many of you in and outside organizations today are anxious. You feel there is something about to drop down on you from above. You might worry about being laid off, fired, or demoted. Or, you may be bored to death doing the same old thing but console yourself by saying, "At least I'm getting paid. Compared to the next guy, I'm doing pretty well." But, are you? *Are you learning or are you stagnating?*

From Words to Working Two Jobs

The time has come for you to listen and refocus, to learn to harness your internal resources. Simply hoping more that times will become easier or working harder at your job, will not protect you from the lay-offs, buyouts, mergers, and restructuring so prevalent in today's organizations. Successful people are working two jobs: One is the position they hold in their daily work, the other is as a "self-leader," as described in Chapter One.

Today, successful people are working two jobs.

*The individual's role is...*taking responsibility for your own worklife growth and job productivity while making a contribution to the organization and your customer. Responsibility includes taking the initiative in your worklife planning, negotiating with management for self-development needs, and recognizing ways in which you can add value to the organization.

*The organization's role is...*joining workers at all levels to support "worklife self-leadership" practices. Joining includes worklife guidance, recognition for experimentation and job performance, and encouragement for ongoing personal and professional learning.

Witnessing Your Life and Learning from It

At various junctures in your life it is necessary to define who you are, assess the choices you're considering, and better understand where you're going. You've most likely heard someone say, "There is a book inside everyone." I believe this is true. Everybody's lifetime—her or his journey—is a series of events and stories that can be configured into chapters with a central theme. Sit down and think about the *texture* of your life. I believe that each of you will see and experience vibrant colors. Beth, a former executive with a travel company, said, "Mine are a rainbow of pastels. They represent the diverse groups that I've worked with throughout the world. Whatever I do next must continue to include my interest in different types of people." What colors come to mind when you think about your worklife? What are your loving and painful episodes, your mysterious and uncertain times, your unanswered questions? Your stimulating conversations, your unexpected changes? Your peak productivity? Few of us choose to write autobiographically; others, like Patricia, keep a journal; some read *about* others, finding satisfaction therein; and some of us aspire to a day when we might put pen to paper.

During Patricia's transition, some of the questions that I suggested she explore in her journal included:

- ≣ Name some things that you truly love to do? Go back to when you were a child. Don't sensor your thoughts. Write about what has given you joy.
- ≣ What are some of your qualities and skills that you'd like to use more at work?
- ≣ When have you been most frustrated in your work? When have you felt most stuck?
- ≣ If you had enough money to take care of what you need, what would you consider doing for work? Why this choice?

In this chapter, I encourage you to see your worklife life and *learn* from it, to *understand* and *explain* what you've seen and experienced. Through talking and writing about your experiences, you'll gain a deeper understanding and own—take pride in—your abilities and uniqueness. Picasso did exactly this, with painting and sculpting as his mediums. It's a lifetime process: Be patient, persistent, and tolerant, and learn from your and others' mistakes and success. Be prepared—take notes along the way.

Too often we are blinded by "doing" and are actually unable to see what we do. We dig a joyless rut and live an unexamined worklife as though someone or something else is in control. It's a struggle to sit still and reevaluate yourself, especially when you've been rewarded for "doing." Sophia, a finance account executive, said to me, "In another life, I'd be a costume designer." "Sophia," I asked, "what about *this* life?" While you may never write your autobiography, do think about deepening your understanding of who you are, why you do what you do, and what you bring to the world; this is your security. Do "tell your stories." Your stories are vignettes, each containing a beginning, middle, and end. They bring your history to life for yourself and others, and illustrate how your life story can be applied to your desires and to your customers' needs.

Vivian, a human resource manager, wrote this story to clarify for herself why she left her job. It also gave her a tool for succinctly presenting herself to potential employers.

> I chose to join this company because it offered me an opportunity to expand my ideas and build a top-notch human resources organization in a team-oriented atmosphere. After two years, I discovered that I was unable to implement change due to conflicting leadership styles among us. I realized that my priorities were to make decisions and influence the organization's direction. However, I continued to feel blocked and frustrated in my work and I left on good terms.
>
> Next, I joined a management consulting practice but, after a year, I found that I missed dealing directly with internal organizational issues.
>
> Now I am seeking a position where I can influence people personally and successfully design and implement human resource policies and programs that are flexible and tailored to meet diverse worker needs and organizational goals.

In my grandfather's day, people would sit for long hours telling one another stories about the Old Country. If they ran out of stories, they listened to the radio. Storytelling was an expression of the texture and fiber of their lives—work, family, and social endeavors. Storytelling helped them understand their times, share what they did, appreciate one another, and seed the future with their history.

To begin telling *your* stories, I encourage each of you to identify positive life or work experiences, one or two from childhood and adolescence and three or four from adulthood. Here are five questions you might ask yourself:

1. What challenge did I face and what did I do to solve the problem?
2. What skills and personal qualities did I demonstrate in meeting this challenge?
3. What was the outcome?
4. What did I enjoy about the experience and how did I benefit from it?
5. How did I benefit others by solving this problem?

Rather than telling and writing your own story, ask a friend to write down your story as you describe your experiences. Have your friend read back what you have said. You could also tape record your story and play it back. Whichever option you choose, listen to your story; it is filled with valuable information about what you enjoy, what you do well, and how you do what you do. This information will help you better see and experience yourself. It is vital for your security—your personal growth and worklife mobility.

Before attempting to tell and write their stories, many of my clients say, "I've contacted 50 people, but nothing is happening," "I'm not sure what to do next," or "I've done lots of things, but so what?" I often respond by asking, "Do you know what you want now? Do you know what you bring to today's workplace?" I explain that if they don't know the answers to these questions, then they'll be wasting energies and creating needless frustration for themselves. One of my clients, Kerry, a news commentator and radio talk show host, said, "I'm having trouble putting together a resume. I'm confused and unfocused; I have too much information to sort through." I asked him, "Can you name three skills—only three—that you want to bring into the marketplace?" He looked relieved; my question provided focus and he was able to name three skills. Subsequently, Kerry shared several stories with me about his accomplishments. These stories reinforced and supported his skills and provided information that we incorporated into his resume.

You Can Commit to Continuous Learning

Compare the items in the two columns below and note the characteristics that best describe your commitment to learning.

Hold on to the Past	*Engage in Continuous Learning*
Deny that things have changed; believe that others need to change but not you.	Notice how you and the environment are changing; believe that you can learn how, regardless of your age.
Ignore your feelings about change; spend your energies squelching your anxiety.	Talk with others about how you're feeling about personal change and the changes around you.
Defend what you do and how you do it as the best or only way.	Stay open to the possibility that you can learn new methods, improve your performance, and increase your productivity.
Depend on others to manage your career.	Become a career self-manager; initiate and plan your learning.
Stay confined to your title.	Rewrite your job description or your career goal and propose a new title.
Try to do only what you want to do.	Examine what you want and how it is relevant to the needs of others.

Glued to Your Title?

Kerry wanted a different challenge. His title, news commentator and radio talk show host, no longer reflected who he was and what he wanted to do. He had a new goal: to work with a national television station as a news reporter and commentator. Your title—employment manager, programmer, vice president of finance—may also represent a confining box. In another era your title worked; at present, however, it may not be serving you or the marketplace. Your title is only a temporary creation designed as an appendage for meeting ego, organizational, and customers' needs. What's behind your title? What do you *now* bring and what do you want to bring to your customers? That's what we all need to know and what our customers will buy. Every successful "self-employed" person knows this.

Job titles, along with jobs, are being eliminated. Caught in the middle of most large organizations, for example, the "manager of" is a victim of the trend toward advanced information systems and flatter organizational structures. As a result, many have reshaped their careers and retitled themselves. Kerry did the same; he traded "holding on to the past" for "continuous learning" and considered the tradeoffs shown on the previous page.

Letting go of your title and creating another is often a confusing and painful process. Kerry expressed many people's sentiment. "I have this panicky feeling, as though I have nothing to hold on to." Laboring under this ambiguity, doing your current job and/or looking for another job, even if you are voluntarily making a change, and understanding that "you are not your title," are challenges for everybody. Kerry reminded himself continuously, "I am in transition; I'll be OK. Letting go of my title isn't easy, but it is a positive step toward my goal." So often, whether at work, at a party, at lunch, at the grocery store, or at home, people ask us, "What do you do?" Frequently we respond with our title, "I am a..." Doing so is convenient and safe. It has been my experience that if I choose, in lieu of my title, to explain what I do (which actually is much more accurate and meaningful than my title), most people tend not to listen. Their eyes glaze over as if "the process" I engage in is too difficult or takes too much work to comprehend. Listening is hard, but necessary, work.

Confusion and pain, as Kerry discovered, seem to rise as ambiguity increases. Ambiguity is necessary—it's part of the self-assessment process. It comes from "burning the grass" and not knowing what will happen next. Our forebears, as my grandfather, went through this transition. You can too. Others want answers and we are conditioned to give them, or afraid not to. Our challenge is to share our present truth and overcome our fear even if we are uncertain about what we want. Tell people, for example, "I'm in process. What I was doing no longer meets my needs; therefore, I am taking this time to reassess." If they don't understand in the moment, go on. Perhaps someday they will.

I'm beginning to learn and respect that what I'm doing today will likely change tomorrow. Hiding behind the safety of my title masks my growth. What I have to give to people is my "learning about what I know." I can't learn and give what I know if I confine myself to a title—a box. It is limiting. Another solution I have found is to begin the conversation with my title—"career consultant"—and follow with a descriptive phrase—"I'd like to describe what I do. I help individuals inside and outside of organizations assess their strengths, know themselves better, redirect their energies, and increase their productivity." In this way, I satisfy them and me. I can change my description as I evolve and the market changes. Moreover, I can also change my title down the road if necessary.

I remind myself and coach my clients, "Your spouse will still love you; your friends will still invite you to play golf; your children will continue to enjoy playing with you; and you can still be as creative and resourceful as you want to be whether you are a lawyer, professor, chef, or vice president. You are not alone in your struggle to get out of the box. The struggle is a necessary part of your growth." To stay glued to your title can be a resignation to your past or a denial of your current work situation. Learning—living—doesn't happen within the boundaries of our titles, a place where our fears can fester. Rather, it occurs in stretching and reconfiguring what we have created or what has been created for us.

I heard on WBUR public radio in Boston that we—the public—allow famous people to "labor under ambiguity." We think it's OK for politicians, movie stars, and presidents to grow and develop, make mistakes, redefine themselves, and contribute all at once. We look up to and need to idolize them. They are different, special. We can learn from them. My suspicion is that many public figures wrestle with ambiguity. You would not have cast your vote or bought your ticket at the box office for them had they not been able to maneuver through the maze of life to get to the polls or the box office and win your heart. They, I imagine, give themselves permission to persevere and overcome the obstacles in order to express their greater purpose. I encourage and support my clients to do the same. Not only can they be derailed by the judgment of others, but as their internal tape plays, many judge themselves. Letting go of your title is not a mechanical process, but an emotional one. It takes time, patience, flexibility, support, and skill—especially when you've been forced to give it up.

Many of us have lived in a square (box)—the symbol for stability and security—and held on to our niche, title, or belief. Many of us also got stuck there. Angeles Arrien, a cross-cultural anthropologist, said, "Symbols are the universal language. They bridge the invisible worlds with the visible worlds. The decades of the 1990s and going into 2000 will be a time of learning how to walk the mystical [independent and interdependent] path with practical feet, how to have a leg in both worlds, the inner and the outer."

That means we will abandon the square for the triangle—emphasizing cooperation and synthesis. We will rely more on passion and purpose, on skills and values. This ability is what organizations and customers will buy, not your title. The following "action-results statement" illustrates this point:

I wrote (action verb) an article for Fortune magazine about collaboration in the workplace, which resulted in receiving an invitation from a division vice president to submit a proposal to do team building for a group of senior executives.

This is an active statement that presents what you do or did, as opposed to presenting your title, "I'm a project manager." Your title, represented by the square, won't suffice anymore. It boxes you into the past. It constrains your mobility. In the following pages, you'll find the definition of an action-results statement, a guide to writing your own such statement, and examples of action-results statements. Whether you work in a company full- or part-time, own a business, or are looking for your first job, action-results statements can help you articulate your talents, skills, and experiences as a means of expressing who you are, what you have done, and how you can add value to an organization or a customer.

The Action-Results Statement: A Definition

An action-results statement is clear and concise. Its purpose is to help you clarify and understand your capabilities and articulate them to others. For your job productivity and career mobility, the statement can be organized into tools such as a "capabilities and accomplishments statement," a marketing letter, or a personal biography.

The Action-Results Statement: A Guide to Writing Your Own

An action-results statement has three parts. It begins with an action word or verb. This word represents one of your skills, such as *presented.* Next, it describes what you did and for whom, such as *a core mid-management training program that highlighted team building and leadership development.* Finally, it states outcomes or results, as in *resulted in 95 percent participation and the delivery of the same program to other managers.*

Put the three parts together to complete the statement:

Presented a core mid-management training program that highlighted team building and leadership development, and resulted in 95 percent participation and the delivery of the same program to other managers

Try writing one action-results statement using the above example above as a guideline. A simple way of identifying your skills and their effectiveness is to tell a friend a story about one of your accomplishments and how you achieved it. Ask your friend to write down skills and action phrases as you tell your story. Use this to begin writing other action-results statements.

The Action-Results Statement: Examples

These statements were written by individuals who work in a variety of professions and who were actively involved in enhancing their current job or seeking a different job. Note that each statement is composed of three parts: 1) an action word, 2) a description of what was done and for whom, and 3) the outcomes or results.

- **Coached** sales representatives and managers on specific sales situations, including overcoming buyer resistance and cold-call rejection, resulting in advancing selling skills, retaining clients, and increasing business
  —*Business consultant*

- **Designed and communicated** corporate benefits package, including payroll-based, executive, work and family, and international benefit plans, leading to current packages that meet worker/employer needs
  —*Manager, benefits planning*

- **Promoted** employee involvement as part of an overall quality and productivity improvement strategy. As a result, over 200 quality circles were established companywide.
  —*Director, staff development*

- **Directed** the formation and execution of an expert system-based problem diagnostic tool, resulting in a 55 percent improvement in diagnostic time and cost
  —*Reliability manager*

A Case Study

To make the transition from news commentator and radio talk-show host to national television news, Kerry decided to construct his action-results statements differently. He turned them around into *results-action statements*. In the media world, Kerry's customers wanted to hear, quickly, what he had accomplished. Kerry said, "To get my foot in the door, I need to be able to speak their language. Presenting my accomplishments first and then following with the way I achieved them is a better way to get their attention."

Here are some examples of statements Kerry presented to potential employers:

- *Ratings increased by 25 percent during the last year* due to the unusual guests I recruited for my show, the timing of the show, and my interviewing style.
- *I was awarded several commendations from the president of the station* for timely reporting and in-depth interviewing.
- *I received a personal letter from a foreign world leader* for "gracefully and tactfully handling delicate issues" in a recent interview with him.

The Struggle to Move from the Box to the Triangle

Analyzing what you specifically do, writing about what you do, letting go of the parts of your work that you've grown beyond, and then deciding what you want to market can be extremely frustrating and bring forward unexpected feelings. It is rarely without resistance that people put aside their title and go about the process of analyzing, evaluating, and writing about what they do. Zoe, a former private-high school dean, wanted to move to an arena in which she could lead and counsel others and earn more money. She began by competently and enthusiastically immersing herself into the inner work—clarifying her skills and values and delving into understanding better her passion and purpose. Her self-discovery unfolded through answering questions, writing, and sharing her thoughts with me. Then came the outer work—exploring where and how her past experiences and current desires might align with the marketplace—coupled with her resistance. Eyes staring intently into the corner of my office, Zoe seemed frozen in place as I shared the process of networking with her. After several moments, she said, "My current title has prestige. I've enjoyed some of the special treatment that has come along with it. As I imagine exploring the business world, where I'll likely earn more, I know that I won't be able to start at the top of an organization. How will I cope with this change? I wonder [if] I really want to make this switch." Zoe's feelings about, and questioning of, transition are common and must be considered as her journey unfolds.

Letting go of a work title that is no longer representative of what one does or wants to do is demonstrated in the case of Martin, a programmer. Previously Martin spent little time at the computer; now he is called on by division managers to consult with them on technical problems. Martin's programming job has evolved into technical consulting and his title has changed accordingly, from programmer to technical consultant.

Although this "consultant" felt passionate about his new role, he still disliked his job. As we analyzed the situation together, he discovered that it was not the job he disliked but the lack of recognition he received in his consulting role. "Programmer" no longer fit; "technical consultant" did. Following the principle that "we are all self-employed," Martin took control of his worklife. First, he wrote 10 action-results statements to document what he actually did for work. Martin chose the action-results format because his priority as a consultant was how he did his job. We then role played to familiarize him with talking about his new role. Soon after he initiated a conversation with his boss, during which Martin elaborated on his new role, pointing to its virtues both to the organization and to himself. He spoke of how his current job title was a misrepresentation of his "consultant" status. Martin saw himself differently and so his boss began to see him in a different light—as a "technical consultant." This is a fitting title, at least for now.

Many of my clients say, "It's lonely." Some report, "It's boring when I analyze myself, but I'm good at helping others to." Others admit, "I'm afraid of discovering that I won't have much to offer out of the context of my current work." And many exclaim, "Why can't I sell my title and the list of my skills? I've always found work that way before!"

If you are looking for just "a job"—a put-food-on-the-table type of job—selling your title and a list of your skills *may* work. But if you want more, to uncover your authentic self and live your passion, then telling your story and examining what you do and how you do it is essential. Three obstacles frequently arise for my clients during the transitional process: fear of change *despite* a stated desire for change, lack of knowledge about the current realities of the workplace, and impatience with themselves and/or others.

Zero Debt—A Runway for Meaningful Worklife

Catherine is looking for more than just a job. "I'd like to tell you what my husband and I have decided to do," Catherine began as we sipped coffee. She continued, "First, I'm leaving the high-tech world. I've been in three large high-tech companies and the fourth, a small start-up. The start-up lost its funding and dissolved, and I hit the wall that I needed to in order to move on in my life. We've decided to sell our house. We don't need the granite counter tops and the cobblestone driveway anymore. They were nice for a while [but] now they don't mean much. We want to establish a debt free foundation so that I'm able to worry less about finances and recreate myself."

I asked, "How risky does your decision feel?" Catherine responded, "The toughest part was letting go of the stigma associated with being out of work. You know, 'What would my neighbors think?' We don't have to sell our house. I want to. The time is right for us to live life differently. Finally I've decided to walk the dog at 11:00 in the morning, and I [don't] care what the neighbors [think]. This was a big hurtle for me."

"What else have you let go of?" I asked. As Catherine smiled and leaned closer to me, she said, "I gave up the lease on the BWM. We're selling our furniture. And the membership to the exclusive yacht club, we're giving that up too. In the process of giving up these things, I'm realizing that we can completely start a new life. We can completely start a new life!"

"So what's your worklife goal now?" I asked. "To live with zero debt. Zero debt is our security base." Catherine said. "And we'd like to move to the country where we can feel freer and where I can become an entrepreneur. I'm exploring an on-site concierge service for animals. I'll visit people's homes to take care of their horses, dogs, and cats. I'm not sure if this business will be the one; I'm exploring...my plan has white space. As I say all of this, I haven't given away all my business suits yet."

I said, "You don't have to give them all away. Save a few of your favorites. You never know where 'zero debt,' your passion and ability to change, and your competence might take you."

Risk

Risk is a critical element to developing and managing your career. Colleen, vice president of human resources at sporting goods manufacturer, says, "I constantly ask people what they learned from this or that experience. I encourage people not to judge based on one short-term interaction but to learn from it and incorporate their action into the larger scheme of things."

Learning has no end, but many beginnings. I often hear from people who are working, from those who have lost their jobs, and from those between jobs who lack "focus" or "direction." As Robert Frost said, you must be willing to be "lost enough to find yourself." You may be afraid, rightfully so, especially if you question your ability to find yourself, have had little practice in self-examination, or are impatient with your process. This, I believe, is the case for most of us. We lack practice and patience, and/or deny what is natural: personal and world change. Just because evolution is a natural, we don't necessarily know *how* to grow. Every one of us, though, has a choice: to *learn* that these realities deserve our respect and that we must learn from them or to play it safe—isolate ourselves, climb career ladders, and wait for opportunities to knock.

Few of us feel the permission to risk—a necessary time of learning and of discovery and rediscovery. Excuses will not work in today's demanding workplace, which leaves us with the responsibility for analyzing problems, confronting issues, and resolving them. It is time to view risk as a "learning runway," necessary for the takeoff toward new possibilities.

On the runway, there are no guarantees. You might take off or you might not. If you do take off, to where and to what height? If you don't, then what? Many of you are taking a risk by reading this and thinking about and testing the notion that we are all self-employed. You are learning (questioning, researching, experimenting, and evaluating), giving up some old ways of thinking, and acting and adopting new ways of looking at yourselves.

Using Paradox

Paradoxes contain a truth about living authentically and productively. To my grandfather's neighbors, burning the grass seemed unproductive and chaotic. But to my grandfather it represented growth—each season the grass grew back greener. The following stories demonstrate how four of my clients used paradox in their attempts to forge new directions.

Paradox 1: Risk is Safety

Priscilla, a software networks engineer, was fired from her job and soon after found a similar job in a small, fast-growing company. At first Karen, her new boss, collaborated with Priscilla by talking over plans and asking for her input before implementing them. But, "After a few weeks," Priscilla said, "Karen's questions suddenly turned into demands. She would simply say, 'Get it done by Friday.'" Priscilla was afraid to lose her job again and tried to deny her hurt feelings about being excluded from the planning process. After another month, she admitted, "I have this insidious feeling that I might be fired again. Maybe I'm still feeling the trauma from the last time." I proposed that Priscilla take a risk and confront her fear by sharing her feelings with her boss.

When Priscilla met with Karen, she said, "I'm here because I value our relationship. When I started this job, I felt included in the planning process; you sought my opinions and we were meeting our goals. In the past month, though, things have changed. I'm feeling excluded. I'm ordered to do things. Could we talk about the reasons for the change?"

Rather than playing it safe, Priscilla took a risk. She shared her feelings and didn't make an accusation or demand. Karen told Priscilla about the pressure she was under as a new manager. Together, they talked about ways in which they could support each other.

Paradox 2: Self-employment is Employability

Over the past three years, Lois, a medical documentation project manager, has contributed significantly to increasing sales in the small consulting firm for which she works. She not only developed manuals that satisfied clients' training and information needs but she also managed project teams and developed several new accounts. Then Roger, the new vice president of marketing, offered Lois a 10 percent raise and a revised contract. Roger wanted to partner with Lois in an all-out effort to expand the firm's client base.

Lois neither signed the contract nor accepted the raise. At her next meeting with me, however, she talked about how hard she had worked during the past three years and commented, "I'm angry that I've been given a 10 percent raise. It's standard, which basically means I'm not being seen for my accomplishments and ability. In their eyes, I'm just an employee. I don't feel like an employee; I've helped the business to grow and I've brought in customers."

I responded, "Let's work at deepening your understanding of 'self-employment.' [This] will help you to increase your employability." I suggested that Lois think about Kirby Timmons' phrase, "I'm my own employer. My company is my customer." Lois listened carefully, became curious, and asked, "How can I apply this idea to my situation?" Knowing Lois's excellent performance record, her enthusiasm, and the firm's stage of growth, I suggested that she write her own contract and include an incentive plan modeled after those developed in other, more mature consulting firms. Lois said, "That's right! Roger is my customer and I'm my own employer. I've been satisfying the firm's needs and this is an opportunity to reestablish my relationship with a good customer."

Lois asked Roger for a three-week period to think about the contract and the incentive plan. She was committed to her job and to researching the incentive compensation plans offered by other consulting businesses. She planned to present her own proposal and incentive plan to Roger that would include the results of her thorough research, documentation of her past achievements, and a concise outline of how she would contribute to the firm's expansion strategy. Lois remarked, "If I don't act on the notion that self-employment is employability, I'll probably be unhappy and less productive. Eventually, if I don't choose to leave...who knows? I'd likely get fired anyway."

Paradox 3: Winter is a Time of Growth

It is winter as I write this. The earth appears bleak—snow-covered ground, bare trees, and a cloudy sky. But I remind myself that underneath the snow spring percolates—growth is happening—and I remind my clients, too. The soil and trees are storing nutrients and preparing for warmth. Behind the clouds the sun shines. A client of mine, Dennis, a state government administrator, left his job. "I needed to recharge, and work was not the place. I was in a rut and lost my enthusiasm," Dennis remarked. Although he had savings, he was out of work. To others it looked like he was simply sitting around wasting his time. Dennis's friends and family had difficulty understanding and accepting his behavior. Dennis said, "My wife says, 'Get a job. You've been out of work for two months.' My response to her has been, 'I've been working non-stop for 25 years. I need to rethink things.'"

Dennis has been meeting with me for support and encouragement to use his "winter as a time of growth." Neither he nor I can always tell what is happening, but we both know it is a productive time. Dennis takes long walks, plays racquetball with his friends, enjoys being with his children, reads, and sometimes sits and does nothing. He is not depressed; he is learning from the winter. He is learning to say, "I'm using this time to think about my skills and interests—my life—and the form my future takes is yet to be determined." Winter always leads to spring!

Paradox 4: Your Growth is a Contribution to Others

"I feel it's selfish to spend this time learning about who I am," remarked Grace, a grant writer. Grace has earned two master's degrees and has worked for the past 15 years in several part-time jobs—planner, management consultant, fund raiser, and field work supervisor—while raising two children. Her children are more independent now, but saving for college tuition is fast becoming a priority. Grace feels a personal need to fully apply her education and passion toward helping others. "My husband and family just want me to get a full-time job," Grace said, "but I don't seem to be able to do that. I'm at the stage in my life when I need to figure out what I really want. I feel guilty doing this. Also, over the years, I've lost some of my professional self-confidence. I'd be competing with some very talented people who have been dedicated to their work."

Grace's greatest problem is herself. In the past, she always took the first job offered. This time, although she vowed to plan and assess before she made any commitment, she needed my guidance to stay on course. I said to Grace, "You are talented, well educated, multilingual, and have superior communication skills. This is the time to give yourself permission to understand better how you want to harness your attributes and discover how they are relevant to the marketplace. Your self-awareness is your contribution to others and to yourself."

Grace has scheduled several informational interviews with former colleagues and associates to become reacquainted with them and the current work world. In these meetings, she will seek only information. One question she will ask is, "I am here because I trust your opinion. From your point of view, what do you believe are my three best assets?" After Grace meets with about seven of her contacts, a theme or template may begin to emerge about how others see her and how she might contribute to the world. Through their feedback, she will be better able to harness her skills and contribute to others.

At first glance, the four paradoxes explored above may seem confusing. Yet, they represent some of the deepest, most difficult aspects of changing ourselves and our view of the world. The rewards of embracing a paradox usually far outweigh the cost.

The Evolutionary Rule of Transition

Transition has always been part of our organizational and individual evolution. We often don't see it because we are in it. My grandfather, for example, somehow understood transitions—he would step back, walk slowly (he didn't let anyone push him), and do what he thought was right. He knew that shades of black and white thinking camouflaged the positive aspects of transition, but he also could envision the rewards of moving through it. He lived through the recession of 1907, the depression of 1929, both world wars, and the Korean conflict. Through them he struggled, eventually prospered, and laid down the seeds for the next generation.

Transition is a rite of passage. It's the process of growth from one form to another. It's manifested in the changes from adolescence to adulthood, from single life to marriage. It's the evolution of an agricultural to a manufacturing economy or an autocratic state to a democratic government. It's the transformation of a fledgling start-up to a bustling mid-size enterprise.

Learning and Transition Guidelines

As you reframe your worklife you will at times feel confused and anxious. These are inescapable characteristics of learning and transition. You won't always know all the answers (remember Rilke's words), nor will you be expected to have all the answers. Here are some ways to help yourself:

- **Don't Push. Do participate.** You'll learn as you think about your past, answer questions, hear from others, and plan for the future.

- **Don't Panic.** This is an opportunity to figure out what you want and how you can be more productive in and outside your organization.

- **Expect Discomfort.** Distress is not a sign, necessarily, that something has gone wrong, but that something is changing. During any transition, it is common to feel anxious—to feel both threatened and excited by new possibilities. Exercising, talking with a trusted colleague or friend, and writing in a journal can help you manage stress and anxiety.

- **Continue Learning.** Your ability to risk and learn has brought you to this point. Continue—give yourself permission and time to learn new things.

- **Take Care of Yourself.** Do little things that make you feel good. Take walks, read, or watch your favorite TV programs. Don't force change—take breaks.

≡ **Allow for Spilled Milk.** When I plan, I find that my plans vary. They range from daily to-do work lists to writing down the five stages for painting the backyard fence to preparing for a client session or presentation. In each case, my plan takes a backseat to the process. My mood, an e-mail, a telephone call, or an unexpected event can derail my priorities and rearrange my plans. Last summer, when I was preparing the backyard fence for painting, my daughter Gabriella and assistant, spilled a glass of milk on the patio. I grabbed the hose to wash down the table and the deck and then, curiously, changed the nozzle setting to full action. I directed the force toward the fence and voila, miraculously, paint shreds began flying off! My plan, to scrape the fence, suddenly changed to a less strenuous and quicker method. As I write, I learn more about what I'm writing about, and this learning becomes the truer content. I've learned that a good plan initiates a process and spilled milk improves it!

Respect Your Inner Voice

It's been a long haul for Anne, a nursing director. During most of her worklife she has felt that she has compromised her true abilities. She has worked *for* her bosses, never considering any other possibilities. At her most recent job, her boss was a detail person; you know the type, cross the *t*s and dot the *i*s. Anne's personality is at the other end of the spectrum. Although she respects the need for detail, she is a big-picture person—someone who creates a vision and takes action by clearly defining the necessary steps and guiding and managing others toward reaching the goal. In other words, she is a manager *and* a leader.

Anne's inner voice, buried under years of compromise, often whispers to her, "I am a leader." When her boss left the medical institution for another job, Anne took this event as a cue to seek a career consulta-tion with me "to listen to my inner voice, to tell others, 'I am a leader.'" Anne's meetings with me were an opportunity for her to learn from her past. Her goals were to understand her true abilities and learn how she could become her own best advocate for doing work that more closely represented who she was and what she had to contribute.

I asked Anne, "What would be the purpose of listening to your inner voice?" Enthusiastically, she responded, "To become more familiar with my natural abilities; to name what they are. I want to strengthen my conviction so that I can become a candidate for an internal position as vice president of nursing...a leadership position." Anne spent several sessions discussing her past. She told me stories about her abilities in three primary areas: leadership, management, and internal consulting.

> **Leadership.** Generally, I believe my role is to develop staff and all other workers who are committed to care. One way that I fol-lowed through on this vision was to create and develop monthly educational seminars to help staff understand the chronic pain of cancer patients. I also encouraged one of the chief physicians, Alan, to join me in an effort to form a new position and establish funding for a half-time chronic pain expert. With his advocacy skills and my ability to sell the idea to different departments, including the chronic pain unit, we now have a part-time expert who aids patients and educates staff.
>
> **Management.** I changed the staffing structure of an inpatient set-ting and reduced management from four to two. This was a good example of my ability to negotiate with staff and union members. I showed my concern for those who would be losing their jobs, and I put the facts on the table: we needed more direct primary

care, not more management. After some debate, we substituted two managers for three primary-care staff.

Consultation. Through in-depth, face-to-face interviewing, I surveyed 30 professional staff members in 8 different medical facilities to gather information about their ethical concerns and their interpretations of the patient's right to choose treatment. My staff and I compiled the data, and I presented the findings to the board of our facility.

In the process of telling her story, Anne explained, understood, and owned her abilities. Her voice deepened, her posture became more erect, and she smiled confidently. She developed a self-employed attitude. She said, "If I don't get the vice president position, I'll be prepared to look elsewhere for a leadership position." Anne learned that at any point in her career she could always respect the texture of her inner voice.

Gracefully Bold

If you've attended to your inner voice, your outer voice will change as a result. It will become more flexible and stronger, but not brash. Holly, a labor relations specialist, noted, "As I talk about what I've done, I'm developing the confidence to become gracefully bold. I tell people what I can do and what I can't or don't want to do without beating them over the head with my accomplishments or my preferences."

To enhance your career or attract new customers, you must know yourself and be able to articulate how what you offer meets another's needs. Most professionals have never had to tell their stories or present themselves as service providers. In the past job market, skills or products were accepted at face value—high-tech, real estate, finance. *Grace* is knowing yourself. To be *bold* is to express your authentic self in such a way that you are serving others and yourself. This is a new and challenging concept but one that is crucial for surviving now and thriving in the future.

Learning from and Reframing Your Mistakes

Developing a self-employed attitude is a process that requires you to learn from your mistakes. Sometimes people go kicking and screaming from limbo into their reassessment stage. Thomas, an events coordinator and consultant at a nonprofit agency, took a job working *for* an authoritarian boss, Clark, who blames others when anything goes wrong and rarely respects the opinion of staff unless that opinion is closely aligned with his own. During the job interviews, Clark said, "I encourage others to share their opinions" and "People get a lot of latitude around here for trying different ways of doing things." Thomas accepted the position because he liked what Clark said.

Within two weeks, Thomas reported, "I discovered that Clark did not 'walk his talk.' He berated staff who shared their own ideas and although we [have] not had a confrontation yet, I [know] that my independent style would not jibe with his." Thomas is responsible—in his words, "overly responsible." He is the kind of person who likes to be given a general picture of what needs to be done. He then organizes himself, plans out the events, and completes the project on time. This was not good enough for his boss, however. Clark wanted Thomas to do things his way. As time went on Thomas discovered that other staff members felt blocked as well but were keeping their mouths shut. Most of the staff were there to meet their own needs although initially many of them, like Thomas, had joined because they believed in the mission of the agency.

There was plenty of "dirt" on the floor but everyone was stepping over it, too afraid to confront the issues and the boss. Thomas would not compromise his values. "I'm a straight shooter!" Thomas exclaimed. "One of my talents is to *notice* what is going on and *do* something about it. I'm living a lie not to be my independent self—to say what's on my mind and help the cause."

Over a six-month period, Thomas and Clark had many opportunities to talk. Thomas felt that he was unfairly judged most of the time, the more he vied for his independence—to contribute in his way— the more punitive Clark became. Eventually, Thomas and Clark reached an impasse. Clark asked Thomas to resign and offered him a one-month severance package.

Thomas was angry and his ego was a little bruised because he hadn't submitted his resignation *first*. In our sessions he yelled, "I couldn't stand the dirt on the floor!" He repeated this phrase several times. Once he vented his anger, Thomas recognized that "seeing the dirt on the floor" was one of his *assets*—an asset that he had honed over the years. I said to him, "Let's do some reframing. 'Seeing the dirt on the floor' means to me that you have an ability to see what the issues are and to give people feedback so that they can grow." Thomas's eyes lit up and I asked, "Is this true?" "Yes," Thomas responded. "It's been the case throughout my life." I explained to Thomas that many people are paid to use this skill—counselors, psychologists, and other consultants. They are compensated for their insight and boldness. Over the next couple of sessions Thomas told me how he had used this skill in a variety of instances. At his last job, for example, he gave feedback to managers about their coaching style with staff members. Now Thomas works *with* a management consulting firm. He is independent—using his best skills—and interdependent—working with a team in which there is a mutual sense of value and purpose.

Honor Your Style

Thomas was asked to resign; in other terms, he was fired. Initially, this was a mixed blessing. Thomas was ready for a change. During his three-month period of unemployment, he transformed himself from adapting and surviving to creating and succeeding. The roots of his change were deeply embedded in his style—or the patterns that best represented what he believed and the ways he performed his work. Thomas is an expressive person who needs to share his opinion and use his creativity to influence others. The best word that I can think of to describe what Thomas felt and what other people like him feel when they are aware of and act on their style is *liberated*. They experience surges of energy and a sense of freedom to overcome everyday obstacles in pursuit of meaningful goals. This does not mean that they are all of a sudden on easy street. On the contrary, your style and the expression of it is a responsibility. It is work and it is a joy. It represents newfound power. The next questions for Thomas—and maybe for you—are, "How are you going to harness your power? For what purpose?"

Once you have found the words to express your style and you begin your search for meaningful work, it is almost impossible to turn back, although you may try. The truth is difficult to avoid. It is not uncommon to have fits and starts. To overcome obstacles and continue on your journey, I recommend that you build a "success and survival kit." Be sure to include in your kit people who will listen to you. You'll know people are listening when you are affirmed for your feelings and supported for doing what you need to do to press on in your worklife—

job, career, and life. A good listener might also make suggestions with your best interests in mind. People who are poor listeners will try to tell you who you are or what you *should* do next. Remember, that's your job. Are there people you trust who might be helpful to you?

Your Success and Survival Kit

A success and survival kit contains the tools (worklife exercises, books, computer, brochures), people, and other support systems that are helpful to you as you go through transition or when you're about to make a work or life change. Your kit might include your spouse, best friend, a specific publication, a journal, a counselor, or a special place where you go to think. Be creative; anyone or anything that is helpful to you can be included in your kit.

On a sheet of paper or in your personal journal, write down who and/or what is in your success and survival kit. You can always change the contents of your kit and most likely you will. Consider the following questions:

1. Which trusted people might be helpful to you?

2. Which things might be helpful to you?

3. Where do you like to go to think and renew yourself?

Loaning Yourself to the Organization

Not only are you the worker in transition, but your company probably is, too. Here's how to deal with both things at once. Your organization may be in the process of making radical changes, redesigning its products and services, or redefining how it will do business. It could also be that your organization is now the right "working" size and structure—it has fewer layers and workers who seem ready to produce. The organization, at least on the surface, is redeveloping and getting ready for business. But are you?

You might be. But more likely you've been working diligently—with your head down—throughout all the changes. Be careful not to bury yourself in the tasks at hand. Remember the bigger picture. Remember, your success and survival—and the organization's—are at stake. No one individual or organization can always foresee or precisely control outcomes. "I've got a good situation," commented Janice, an advertising account executive, "but we could lose a major deal and my job could be at stake." Reframe your work situation. Take an hour a week to schedule a meeting with yourself to do just that. If you're developing a "self-employed" attitude, remind yourself that you're loaning yourself and your expertise to this organization for a period of time.

Thinking this way can be liberating, even if you're not sure how it translates to the marketplace. Jobs may be scarce in your field, but what remains is the nature of today's work world. You'll have a job only for as long as you are providing a service—something that adds value within a niche that's yours—that someone will pay for. Knowing this, you can do your job and keep your eyes open for alternatives.

Personal redeveloping involves doing comprehensive research to make prudent worklife and business decisions. Therefore, if you're thinking about leaving your organization, you must thoroughly examine your reasons and options. One consideration, often unrecognized, is that moving on doesn't have to mean leaving your organization. You have made an investment in your current organization, including the time you've spent getting to know the culture and colleagues, sharing your expertise, and contributing your knowledge. Realistically, if you do leave you would still be responsible for your job productivity and career mobility. There are no guarantees anywhere; you would still be self-employed, no matter what you decide.

What Value Do I Add to Your Worklife?

As a regular part of my clients' exploratory worklife processes, I encourage them to ask six to eight trusted colleagues and friends, inside and outside or work, the following question: "What value do I add to your worklife?" The purpose of this question is to generate honest feedback to enhance self-esteem and decision-making ability, and to increase mobility and productivity. Asking six to eight participants, typically, gives a broad enough survey for gathering similar and diverse themes. Initially, you may be reluctant to ask others to participate but my overwhelming experience suggests that most people are delighted to respond. Most are curious and can identify with you; they are in the same boat, have been there before, or can foresee a similar change in their future. Hopefully, you'll take the risk to ask others for their support and be able to take in and absorb their feedback; each has taken time to share their thoughts about you.

Manuel, a university department head, e-mailed the note to seven of his colleagues:

> I think I mentioned to you that I'm working with a career counselor to help me uncover "what" I'd like to do in my next career and then figure out where and how to apply that "what." The process is one of discovery, looking inward to find what passion lies within.
>
> At this point, I've been asked to learn more about me through the reflections of others. Because we have known each other for more than 10 years, your thoughts and opinions mean a lot to me. If you could find a little time to help me on my journey of discovery, I would appreciate it so much.

What I'd like to know is, what value have I added to your life? Or, how has your life benefited from our association and friendship? You can answer professionally, personally, or both. Your answer need not be long and can be as simple as one sentence.

If you choose to participate, please reply by Wednesday, January 22. Thank you for your consideration, time, and thoughts.

Manuel received the following replies from Santo and Danielle.

My life has been going through several "volcanic" changes in the past two years. You have also been experiencing your own earth shaking changes. Not that this is the first time for you either, but I am sure it is one of the most challenging times. During these times, having you in my life has been like sunlight peeking through the clouds after a terrible storm. I have a sense that everything will be fine no matter what. I'm not sure if you give yourself that much confidence about the road ahead in your life, but you have been an anchor for mine. Giving me that strength during the tough time in your own life, I can't help but feel a deep respect and admiration for your energy-giving generosity. Your head may not always be held high—more times than not it is—but nevertheless there is always a sense of not being defeated or giving up.

This is something else that I have drawn my own strength from, to pursue life more aggressively. Your dedication, openness, and love towards others, and [your willingness] to change is empowering to me. I feel that I share those three qualities with you and being around you acts as a "filling station" for my spiritual self. I draw tremendous amounts of enthusiasm, energy, and joy from you.

I could continue, but I feel that what I have said will be all I need to say about how and what you have added to my life. Thank you for being YOU. —Santo

You were important to me because you made me laugh when at times I felt there was not much to smile about. You were also a great sounding board, dispensing levelheaded advice. Over the years I have also admired your independence—you are your own person. How do these things add value? I don't think I can quantify it, but I suppose I would like to look at it in more colorful terms. I view life as a canvas and the people we meet in life make up the colors and brush stokes. I think you would be a beautiful color. —Danielle

After gathering all seven responses, Manuel shared them with me saying, "To be perfectly honest, I'm trying to accept and acknowledge that I am those things that people say."

During our sessions together, Manuel and I will talk about themes and discuss how the feedback from his friends and colleagues feedback can be used in his search. My sense is that through the process Manuel will learn to accept and acknowledge his truth.

Inspiration

Sheila was a training manager at a software company that was eliminating as many managers as possible in an effort to reduce costs and streamline operations. She was the primary financial provider for her family and wondered, "How can I save my job and still be true to who I am?" First, she determined in what specific ways the company was changing. Her analysis revealed that the management training department would be slowly phased out. Sheila clarified and prioritized her core skills and decided that her consulting and project management skills would be valuable in the company's newly structured divisions. She rewrote her job description, presenting herself to her boss as a project manager who would consult with internal and external customers. She reframed her background and created another job in the same organization. Sheila planned to use this job as a bridge toward another position externally in the event that she decided to leave.

The Struggle is Part of the Action

Most of you have been paid to do your jobs, not necessarily to think about and explain to others what you do for work. If you lost your job tomorrow, you would be thrust into the job marketplace or into your workplace's market. You would have to learn to explain clearly what it is that you do and how your skills and abilities apply to a potential organization's or customer's needs. If you no longer wanted to do the same work or if the type of work you had been doing no longer exists, you would be faced with another type of personal renewal puzzle.

Whatever the case, you would want to create your best chance for doing what is you: work that reflects your skills, abilities, values, passion, and purpose. "I don't want to do the same old things; they bore me," claimed Ed, an accountant. "I'm 51 years old. It's time to shift my focus and feel excited about my work again. But this transition is difficult—the old ways no longer fit and I'm unsure about where I'm headed." The struggle is part of personal renewal in action. It's a struggle to sit still and reevaluate yourself, especially when you've been rewarded for doing. Compounding the struggle is the nature of the current competitive and fluctuating job market. These claims bear some truth but, as one of my clients asserted, "You've got to accept the struggle. It's part of getting to where you want to go. I've got to assess and evaluate who I am, what I want, or I'll always be scared about what might happen to me."

**One must still have chaos in oneself to be able
to give birth to a dancing star.**

—Nietzsche

Advancing Your Worklife Goals

We are all self-employed is our new conscious reality but living it doesn't come easily. "The journey is unpredictable," said Lisa, the editor-turned-scriptwriter. "Furthermore," she continued, "there were times when I felt exhausted. Once I started on this path I feared giving up. My greatest fear was that I would end up doing work again just to pay the bills. Understanding myself and pursuing work that I really wanted seemed so elusive at times."

Asking trusted friends and colleagues about the value you have added to their lives can help you understand yourself and add steam to advancing your worklife goals.

Lisa found support and persevered. Now that she is working as a scriptwriter, she is feeling good about her accomplishment. She is challenged to write in a different way, producing scripts that can be adapted to video and DVD. In addition, she is aware that her needs—much like what she is doing today—will change. Having made the move to scriptwriter has given her the confidence to see that she can assess her needs and manifest her goals. And, she can make this process work again.

You cannot assign responsibility for your life to anyone. Life requires integrating self-information that no one else has...both intuitive and factual. You must keep on checking, Is what I'm doing right for me? This is not simple because of internal and external variables.

—Mark Campbell, executive coach

Inviting Myself In

To sustain, renew, or aspire to competitive success, large and small organizations must reassess and change the ways they do and think about work. Many of these organizations have applied methodologies—total quality management (TQM), reengineering, redeveloping, self-managing teamwork—to guide them through radical redesign or toward innovative processes. In fact, these methodologies have become much more than practical applications for solving problems. They have become ideologies—philosophies founded on specific tenets for transforming vision to reality, beliefs that transcend complexity and obstacles in order to achieve specific outcomes. The new systems have given us permission to rethink what we do and the language to communicate how we do what we do.

A new breed of pioneers is helping organizations rediscover themselves and go beyond survival toward success. They have adopted a "self-employed" attitude and are helping their organizational clients do the same. It is to Tom Peters's credit that we now "search for excellence." Peter Senge steers us through a "learning" labyrinth out of the classroom, into the boardroom, and throughout every function in the organization. Margaret Wheatley teaches us that chaos, as we see in nature, is necessary for growth. Robert Reich reminds us to rethink the future of success in our Internet-driven marketplace. Jim Collins explores the virtues of good-to-great companies and he and his research team share their exuberance and their findings with us. These management experts have *invited themselves* into a global marketplace of change. Their timing is right.

Similarly, Len, a divisional general manager at a food manufacturing conglomerate noticed, "The former president used to direct the show and, basically, we would follow. High-priced followers! In contrast, the new president expects the GMs to initiate—share ideas and participate in decision making." From now on, Len will need to recognize problems, suggest where costs can be cut, and decide when to institute new programs or expand on existing ones. With fewer workers, increased workloads, and greater pressure to innovate and perform, Len must learn a new management philosophy and strategy. His learning is not only about how to manage others but also how to manage his own career at work. Len must reconsider how to take personal risks, especially at his level, to sharpen his awareness of what needs to be done and test the relevancy of his ideas.

The closer you are to who you are, the more responsibility, stability, and mobility you have.

Conscious Loneliness is Part of the Journey

Undeniably, every one of us—alone—must face ourselves and the changes that we must make. We can surround ourselves with other people and things in the hope that others will know us better than we know ourselves. Or, we can cling to past beliefs and archaic organizational values and norms, only to one day find that our growth has been retarded, that we have been stymied by our fear of loneliness—as though loneliness is something to be avoided at all cost. In *Man's Search for Himself*, Rollo May comments on the characteristic threat of loneliness:

> When one's customary ways of orienting oneself is threatened, and one is without other selves around one, one is thrown back on inner resources and inner strength, and this is what modern people have neglected to develop. Hence loneliness is a real, not imaginary, threat to many of them.

For a moment, think about a recent change in your worklife and about the inner resources that you used to make this change.

- ≣ What is one activity that you have given up in the past 12 months?
- ≣ What are you doing now instead of this activity?
- ≣ What inner resources did you use to make a successful transition?
- ≣ What would you discover if—just temporarily—you were not distracted by television, friends, colleagues, organizational boundaries, or self-deprecating thoughts?
- ≣ What would you uncover if you took your precious time—10 minutes, two hours, or a weekend—to begin thinking about your life and what you really want?
- ≣ What would happen if you committed to a self-inspired journey that included unavoidable emptiness—fibers woven into the rich texture of the fabric of self-discovery?

With patience, persistence, tolerance, and learning, you can live your life—the process—and achieve goals that are meaningful to you. You can serve yourself and others. You can be happier.

We tend to be alive in the future, not now.

—*Thich Nhat Hanh*

When I think about my own times of loneliness, not aloneness, I am in touch with an "empty" feeling as though I am missing something—as though there is little present when I allow myself to be still, undistracted. After I adjust to the stillness, I can feel my heartbeat, experience air passing in and out of my body, and sometimes I am alarmed at how shallow my breathing is. When I give myself permission to be lonely I walk into the emptiness and don't judge the experience through the lens of our "instamatic" culture. I see myself coming toward myself, as if I am having an out-of-body experience. Objectively, I come to a point of identifying areas in which I need to grow and to accept my need to learn—take risks. I accept my need as growth and life, not as an impediment but as a challenge and a chance to foster my independence. I can see, for example, that I need to follow my own dreams. It is when I try to follow others that I feel most anxious and derailed from myself. When I give myself a chance in the empty, lonely times I eventually find myself in fuller times. As Thomas observed, "I've got to be who I am and do what I need to do." Loneliness happens to be part of the journey for everybody.

Unconscious Loneliness

Rollo May said:

> The clearest picture of the empty life is the suburban man who gets up at the same hour every weekday morning, takes the same train to work in the city, performs the same tasks in the office, lunches in the same place, leaves the same tip for the waitress each day, comes home on the same train each night...and moves through a routine, a mechanical existence year after year until he finally retires at sixty-five and very soon thereafter dies of heart failure, possibly brought on by repressed hostility. I have always had a secret suspicion, however, that he dies of boredom.

As the chains of boredom were strapped on to many workers, our society was slowly being broken; today, that's the way our society *is*. We have no choice but consciousness.

Getting Paid: No Guarantees

A self-employed attitude includes emotional, psychological, philosoph-ical, and social factors. And let's not forget the economic factor—get-ting paid! Incentive compensation is based on results—pay-for-performance. But not all organizations or executives see or respect this system. At a financial services company, the president gathered his top executives for a meeting. The agenda was to discuss compensa-tion. At the time, the executives were paid a guaranteed bonus—an amount, up to a particular percentage, *promised* to each executive beyond his or her salary. The president proposed that the executives consider an incentive compensation package instead. Rather than a guaranteed bonus, the executives were presented an appreciably larger incentive: an opportunity to commit more deeply to joining in the process of running the company, as if they owned a share of the busi-ness. At year's end, the executives' contributions would be judged against predetermined goals. If they met their goals, they would be paid an amount for their contribution and an additional amount based on the performance of the company as a whole. Self-employed work-ers are paid this way and, as many of you know, sometimes they don't get paid at all, or not as much as in previous years. Pay-for-perfor-mance: this is the real world.

In the financial services company discussed above, it is interesting to note that when the ballots were counted the executives chose safety over adventure—that is, to retain the compensation system of guaran-teed bonuses. Their choice may work for them in the short term because the company is doing well but, paradoxically, safety—guaran-teed bonuses—is no longer safety at all. The president had offered his executives a challenge: to look at themselves, to become more account-able for their actions, and to learn a new way to be successful that is in greater harmony with the world. Next time, I believe, these workers won't have a choice. Why should anyone get paid for anything else but performance—doing their job?

To Learn, Learn Something New

At midlife, I resolved to take flute lessons. My decision was made having never held a flute. Also, I could not read a note. A standard measure—a configuration of quarter and half notes—looked like a foreign language. However, in my mind, the flute symbolized challenge and growth.

Opening the instrument's case, I feel excitement. Thinking, "I need to play to perfection," brings up fear and makes me ask myself, "Am I enhancing my own life? Am I a man of learning? Am I creating, or standing by? Is my life fuller in the moment?"

A year into the process now, I've become aware of how I learn best. When I listen to Mies Boet-Whitaker, my flute teacher, I'm inspired. Often, I ask Mies to play a song before I try. Then I can hear in total—and beauty—what I am trying to accomplish. Rather than attempting to play the entire song, I've learned, through my frustration and successes, to play one note and one measure at a time. It's like writing one word, one sentence, and then another to complete a paragraph and eventually a book. When I play a note, I focus on accurately reading it from the music book. Is it a G, a C, or an A? Then I transfer what I see to my breath and fingers. A sweet sound signals, "Try the next note." And if I'm flat or too sharp, I go back to try again.

Most importantly, I've noticed that learning takes practice. *Practice* makes all the difference, not talent. If I get too frustrated or my fingers stiffen and tire, I give myself permission to rest or quit for the day. When I pick up the flute again, I feel renewed and the note, usually, sounds fresher. Like magic, if I practice consistently, my breathing, pace, fingering, tone, and music reading all seem to coordinate effortlessly. My thinking stops and, somehow, my spirit takes over. I have new music in my life and my wife Amy yells from upstairs, "Sounds good!"

Learning something new reveals my pattern of learning. I...

1. Choose something for which I have passion.

2. Find someone, a teacher, to support my learning process.

3. Listen to what the end goal sounds like.

4. Set realistic expectations and goals: take one measure at a time.

5. Practice, consistently.

6. Relax when I get frustrated and try again the next day.

7. Notice, and enjoy, when my thinking stops and my spirit takes over.

8. Pass on my learning.

Gabriella, my eight-year-old daughter, has begun to play the flute. She learned her first four notes from me!

Is it time for you to learn something new? How do you learn best?

Who's the Boss?
Check-In: Beginning the Process of Change with Yourself

1. Do you feel you are learning or are you stagnating? Which "fear" words keep you stagnating in your worklife? With what "freedom" words might you replace them?

2. If you were to describe yourself as a color or colors, which would you choose? Why?

3. I know that you've been rewarded for "doing," but can you sit still now and think about a story that illustrates when you've felt happy and productive in your worklife? Write it down. Share it with a friend. What did you enjoy about the experience? What challenge did you face? How did you benefit others?

4. Are you glued to your title? How do you know if you are "glued" or "unglued?" If you're glued, how might you begin releasing yourself? If you're unglued, how can might you continue your liberation?

5. On a learning runway, there are no guarantees. Still, is it time for you to learn something new in your worklife? What? When will you begin?

CREATING A

MEANINGFUL WORKLIFE

Work and live, believing that the world needs you and that you can make a contribution

EMPLOYED ATTITUDE
Dependent Mindset

What I do doesn't really matter. I'm just doing a job. I bring my body to work and leave my spirit behind.

SELF-EMPLOYED ATTITUDE
Independent and Interdependent Mindset

I will create meaningful work. I am resourceful and able to give value to my work—to market my strengths, negotiate for my needs, and make a contribution regardless of my job or level.

R ight now, you might be overwhelmed. Or, you might be encouraged, asking, "How do I recreate myself? How do I help myself?" I'm not going to give you the answer. I can't. Fulfilling work is about your unique journey and what the world needs from you. Instead, I'm going to share some truths about creating meaningful work that come from my work with clients and my own life experience. I hope the wisdom that I share will lead you toward asking your own questions and seeking your own answers. Most importantly, my wish is that this chapter stirs your imagination and calls you to action—to invigorate your life and to make a contribution to others.

Meaningful Work—a Marathon—and an Occasional Sprint

As I put my meaningful-work skills in motion, I imagine a marathon and, sometimes, I sprint. The sky is a brilliant blue. It is Patriot's Day in Massachusetts and the running of the 103rd Boston Marathon. The international field consists of 15,000 qualified runners. They assemble in Hopkinton, a small town west of Boston, the beginning of the serpentine, 26.2-mile route that traverses seven towns. I stood at mile 19 with over one million other spectators stretched along the route. We applauded and handed out orange wedges and water, as numbers

1158, 1352, and 585 passed by. Many wore the latest running gear and others their favorite "T," some sweated up and down the hills in wheelchairs, a few ran barefoot, and one brave soul clasped walking sticks to propel himself forward. People next to me cheered, "Go, Tina!" "You can make it, Canada!" "Keep going, Kevin." "You're looking too good, Ohio!" Gabriella, a preschooler at the time, threw confetti.

How many of you have run a marathon? Bravo! In my opinion, if you have come to this point in your worklife and you look back on the hills and valleys, you'll see that you've run a different kind of marathon. Congratulations on that.

I was 24 years old when I first ran the Boston Marathon. With youth and exuberance on my side, my goal became to finish without stopping. Not knowing what to expect, the thrill for me was the first-time challenge. At the 18 mile I noticed a clock, saw that I was running two hours strong and broke out into sprint, passing other runners. But my disposition shifted at the 23 mile. My legs cramped and I became dehydrated.

Fatigued, I stretched beyond my physical symptoms, aided by my vision and a voice next to me that said, "Dad, I can't." The father looked and said, "Son, step by step, just one more." I inhaled those words just as the man's son did. We all finished—I, without stopping. To this day, I remind myself "Step by step, just one more."

I greatly value taking on intractable, worthwhile challenges and finishing them. Though if I think about the whole task before me, such as revising this book or playing my flute, I get overwhelmed—drowned in a myriad of thoughts and a multitude of detail. If I listen, become aware of my anxiety, and listen again, I hear "Step by step..." My anxiety, most of the time, is quelled—replaced by enough calm enthusiasm and optimism to focus on the immediate task.

Running the 80th Boston Marathon has been worth to me, personally and professionally, its tally in footsteps. To create meaningful work, I've remembered to expect that: 1) the terrain will shift under my feet, 2) challenges will emerge unexpectedly, and 3) my mood can change as I progress and discover how to adjust as one foot follows the other. Still, I can win my *own* race.

Run Your *Own* Race

Looking at other people's ways of becoming successful can give you clues as to what to do, but you can rarely satisfy yourself or sustain your journey by following in their footsteps. Their dream is not yours. You might try out one of their steps, but don't get caught following *their* path. Each of the marathoners, although surrounded and cheered on by others, ran the distance because he or she was nourished by their own dream.

To run your own race—create meaningful work—here are some of the steps that you might consider:

Look at what you have in your life. I listen to, and empathize with, many whose lives are reconfigured into unfamiliar or perplexing shapes. Rainer, a public relations expert, said, "With more than 17 years of overall marketing communications experience and a track record of success in high tech public relations, I was laid off 13 months ago. Quite unbelievably, I'm still looking for a job at my level. I've been very diligent about networking and sending out resumes but I can't seem to find a position like the one I had. I've pursued other fields and some rather expensive training with the goal of opening my own business, but along the way I've become completely disenchanted. I feel like I'm just floundering. If this isn't a midlife career crisis, I don't know what is."

The first thing that I recommended that Rainer do was to temporarily put his "job seeking" activity on hold and take stock of what he has in his life. I suggested that he begin each statement with the affirmation, "I have..." Rainer's partial list included the following:

I have...

- a supportive loving family.
- the ability to listen to and influence others.
- the ability to think creatively. That's what I've been paid to do and enjoy doing.
- my health and like going to the gym mid-day.
- experience and an education that I can mold and shape to meet my needs and, hopefully, those of others.
- the ability to enjoy the little, simpler things in life: the sound of the crisp snow as I walk through it, the sun that beams through our bedroom window, and the twinkle in my son's eyes as he talks about his school day.

I asked Rainer, "What do you think is the benefit of naming what you have in your life?" He responded, "I leave the zone of desperation and move into a place of thankfulness and positive energy." Reviewing your list often can fortify your journey and make the process even more compelling than your goal.

Take risks even when you don't know where they will lead. Instead of laboring over what will come of your efforts take a course in photography, drawing, hang gliding, or computer technology. As you meet new people you will gather fresh ideas. You can substitute your doubt for hope and trust that your next step will emerge through your personal engagement and interaction with others. Rory, an entrepreneur, sold his business and decided at midlife to explore a path in medieval studies. He's been accepted into a university and is beginning his journey by taking a few courses. I asked, "Where do you think your studies will take you?" Rory replied, "I'm not sure. Since I was a college student I've had interest in this area. Now I'm letting my passion lead."

Step more consciously into what you are doing. Too often it appears that the solution to finding more meaningful work is to stop doing one thing and search for something else to do. This strategy works for many. There are other times, however, when understanding and appreciating the joy in what we are doing now is all that we need to give ourselves. Kendra, an administrative assistant, loves planning, organizing, and scheduling. During her review with Mildred, her boss and a lawyer, Kendra said, "I know that others in the department have been promoted to different positions, and what I have to say may not sound so progressive but I love what I do—systematizing and running the office. I don't want to manage groups or pursue studies in science, medicine, or law. I like being the back-up person...and am good at it." Kendra took control of her career in this moment. She clarified and discussed what was meaningful to her, and she received a five-percent raise.

Milton, a biologist, was asked by his manager Phillip, "Would you like to try managing others?" Like Kendra, Milton responded, "My work isn't done as a biologist, and managing others holds very little interest for me. What is meaningful is nature, exploring new things, [and] scientific discovery."

You can, if the infrastructure will support it, stay where you are and create meaningful work. To support your inquiry and boost your confidence ask, "What do I do best? Do I enjoy it? How do others benefit? Do I want to deepen, and continue doing what I do best?"

Learn from feedback. Valerie, one of the readers of my draft manuscript said, "Arriving at the last chapter, it feels to me as though you ran out of steam. It's not on par with the rest of the book." I thanked Valerie for her feedback and put myself to work with the intent to make the last chapter as inspiring and informative as the rest of the book. Valerie's feedback was a gift calling me to do and offer my best.

Zeke, a management consultant with a specialty in strategic marketing, loved the arts. His dream, so he thought, was to open a gallery that featured original modern art at an affordable price. As he researched the marketplace—interviewed gallery owners—he listened. And when he imagined himself actually running a gallery he tuned into his feelings. The tedium of operating a gallery, Zeke assessed, would not meet his needs for creating strategy and dealing with organizational complexity. And although he continued to feel excitement about modern art, he vacillated, feeling ambivalence—feedback about turning his passion into a business. Now he is exploring strategic marketing opportunities within organizations.

Listen to others and understand their needs. The workplace is a mix of all ages and interests. How does a 50 something person relate to, collaborate with, and sometimes take direction from a 30 something person? How do we communicate across generations? Diana, vice president of store operations, said:

> I ask each of my direct reports, regardless of age, for their opinion.
> I delegate liberally, and get out of the way so that he or she is able
> to perform without me perched over their shoulder. To prepare for
> a team development session, I asked my staff to read *Man's Search
> for Meaning* by Viktor E. Frankl. When we met, each person
> shared his or her insights. I asked a few questions to get things

rolling, then listened to people share their opinions. The idea was to give everyone a chance to value their own thoughts and consider those of others. The trust we build in these meetings, coupled with clarifying goals, and the respect I have for each individual, create common ground and drive our productivity.

Defer gratification, and incrementally work toward your goal. Just as our sessions are about to begin most of my clients ask, "Is it possible to expedite the change process so that I can get back on my feet as quickly as possible?" Others ask, "How long will it take?" These questions are fair. People are anxious to feel secure and productive—know their strengths, create a plan, and land a meaningful job. I often answer, "As the individual moves into the process of discovering who they are and what they want, usually it's my client who presses on the brakes, slowing down to dig more deeply into their questions. And if my client won't pull out of the fast lane, I'll point out that if your process becomes too linear, mechanical, or accelerated, you may overlook vital information that could add immeasurably to consummating a more satisfying job or successful career." I also add, "You might surprise yourself, exceeding your expectations regarding timeline or you might have to flex to alter them. Neither you nor I can precisely predict the time of outcome, but we can engage in a process wholeheartedly with the hopes that you'll know yourself better, understand your options, and develop the attitude and skills to begin a fresh path or deepen the one that you're on."

I recall addressing similar questions with a group of laid-off workers. A gentleman stood up about 10 minutes into the seminar and said, "I don't give two hoots about all this transition and change hoopla. All I want is a job." Facing him and rest of the audience I asked, "Who else wants what this gentleman wants?" Everyone raised his or her hand.

I said, "Obviously, we all want the same thing—to land a good job. To get there, I suggest we talk about our anxiety and that we learn about specific tools that will help us surmount our fears and achieve our goals. Also, not one of us will materialize our goal by acting desperately, for example, by randomly sending out a pile of resumes or cold calling without a plan. We're together so that we can defer knee-jerk activity and engage in a gratifying process that will net results."

Turn your emotions into an asset. Lobsang began our session by reading this quote from Henry David Thoreau, "Most men would feel insulted if it were proposed to employ them in throwing stones over a wall, and then in throwing them back, merely that they might earn their wages. But many are no more worthily employed now." He continued, "For the past several years I have felt locked into 'throwing stones over the wall, and then throwing them back.' Part of my problem is that I've listened to many others share what bothers them and have inspired them to see their own purpose and achieve personal and business goals, but rarely have I been open with them about me." At the end of his sentence Lobsang began to cry. He choked, "I'm embarrassed, and I'm stuck. That's why I'm here." I responded, "Lobsang, you're also here because you want to express your emotion and, knowing you, you'll still want to give to others. You've been an outstanding leader and as you advance in your career you want to grow by sharing more of your authentic self." Lobsang asked, "How does this fit into my purpose, to inspire greatness in others by utilizing creativity and visionary leadership?" "Perfectly," I responded. "Creative and visionary leaders grow and serve others by speaking from their heart. Think about the best speech you've given. Now think about the best speech that you've heard. Were they presented from the heart or the head?" "This is why my tears," Lobsang reflected. "I want to use more of my heart as I lead."

"Yes," I said, "your emotions are an asset. I suggest that you talk with a friend or two to share your purpose and the progress that you've made transitioning. Begin by saying, 'It's difficult for me to talk about myself but I trust you and I'd like to share some things that I've discovered about myself in the past few months."

My suggestion gave Lobsang an opportunity to practice becoming more comfortable with authentically expressing himself in preparation for both interviewing for, and doing, work that resonates with who he has become. Vulnerability is courage at work and can lead to happiness and productivity.

Praise your efforts and take in the praise that others offer you. I discussed earlier the importance of pausing to take stock of what you have in your life. This form of praise represents genuine applause, not Teflon puffery. Praise that sticks, no matter how small or private, is a tribute to you. After my session with Whitney, I emailed her and said, "I'm proud of you. During very uncertain times, you've been able to focus to better understand and articulate your values. I look forward to seeing how you use them and how they guide you in your job search."

I regularly ask clients, "Can you tell me about a few things that you've done that make you feel proud?" Chelsea said, "Now that I've stopped to think about it, in a short time, I've changed the culture within our business by encouraging and facilitating open discussions between executives." Hank said, "I'm feeling good that I'm able to reach out to others during a low point in my life. Just yesterday, I asked a colleague if she would introduce me to someone in her company for an informational interview."

True praise can add traction to your steps. Approval, on the other hand, is a form of dependence. You can avoid getting side tracked by approval if you frame your curiosity within a suggestion such as, "I'm thinking of opening a small restaurant that serves home-cooked meals. My research tells me that people are more health conscious and would prefer baked chicken, a sweet potato, and a mesculan salad to fast food. I know that you live in town, what do you think of my idea?" In this way, you're seeking someone's opinion. If they listen and respond genuinely, their feedback is a gift—a form of praise.

Try easy. Mark Levy, my friend and author of *Accidental Genius: Revolutionize Your Thinking Through Private Writing*, recommends that when we create meaningful work, we "Try easy. That is, the moment you sit down to problem solve, you're to remind yourself that you're not going to be able to banish your ills at once, if ever. You're just going to give a specific problem an enthusiastic shot and whatever you come up with is exactly what you should have come up with. If you don't find the perfect answer, you'll find a bunch of answers, and you'll make one work."

Next, "try easy" again; that is, trust that the step—whether it worked or not—was a teacher. You can learn from it, and your next answer will emerge.

Defy gravity. "Work," said Daniel Levinson in *The Seasons of a Man's Life*, "is of great psychological importance; it is a vehicle for the fulfillment or negation of central aspects of the self." I view this statement as so for women and men. We live in a society where the individual has become increasingly defined by their work and the contribution that she or he makes. Theo, a sales manager, said, "It is unfortunate that so much of my self-esteem is derived from my career."

As individuals we are called, if we want to walk our own path, to challenge the gravitational pull—central stream—of society. I heard this pull the other day from an associate. "Hey," Rob said, "aren't you too old to have an eight year old." I responded, "There's never been a better time in my life."

There's never been a better time than midlife to respect your wisdom, search your experience for clues, and engage your childlike curiosity. Carl Jung, considered the father of the modern study of adult development, found that tremendous opportunity for fundamental change can start at the age of about 40. This can be a time of self-definition and expression and can last for several decades.

Personal gravity, too, can weight your growth and sap your dignity. Frederic Hudson, author of *The Adult Years*, said, "From midlife on, many adults lose their dreams and lock themselves into their memories. As they see it, their best days are behind them." Neither societal nor personal gravity need thrust you into maintenance, decline, or disengagement from life. I think about the words of Marcus Aurelius: "Our life is what our thoughts make it." As I act on the notion, if my mind can think it, the possibility is raised that my body can create it or take me there.

Encouraging my clients to take interim steps helps them defy gravity and move toward their vitality. Doug, an independent financial planner and formerly a real estate developer, studied in the evenings to earn a Chartered Financial Planner (CFP) certificate and worked with the financial planning division of a large bank. To open the doors of her own graphics design business, Ellen first took interim steps designing sets and props for a public TV station. As well, she moonlighted, creating brochures and formatting newsletters for private clients.

Your interim steps can help you explore, build confidence, and gain momentum. At some point, though, living your dream fully requires a leap of faith.

Meaningful Work Steps Review

▤ Look at what you have in your life.

▤ Take risks even when you don't know where they will lead.

▤ Step more consciously into what you are doing.

▤ Learn from feedback.

▤ Listen to others and understand their needs.

▤ Defer gratification, and incrementally work toward your goal.

▤ Turn your emotions into an asset.

▤ Praise your efforts, and take in the praise that others offer you.

▤ Try easy.

▤ Defy gravity.

Meaningful Work and Making a Living

Peter is an award-winning photographer and director of photojournalism at Boston University. His interview below reflects many of the meaningful work steps already discussed. At first glance, Peter struck me as a man with a plan: trim, clean-cut, thoughtful, and focused. Peter talked enthusiastically about his side trips—leaving the plan behind, raising his consciousness about himself and the world around him, and flexing his actions as a means to build his self-confidence, grow his business to earn a six-figure income, and secure a university post. Peter reflects on his self-doubt and how he converted it to faith, learning, and action to pursue meaningful work and earn a living. I hope that you'll be able to borrow a morsel or two from Peter's journey as you fortify your own.

Q: You've been through the unexpected in the past year. Would you summarize your recent journey?

A: I went through many changes over this past year. I wouldn't wish this experience or process on my worst enemy but I know I have come through it with a renewed sense of purpose, more clearly defined priorities, and a confidence I never had before. I started a photography business from square one, and it has succeeded. That in turn has led to a greater sense of interdependence, as you [Cliff] put it, trading in the old dependent model. Success and its accompanying attitude breed more opportunities for greater success, and in my case it has led to a largely unexpected new venture. In addition to a photography business that has succeeded past my most optimistic projections, I am starting a new position as associate professor and director of the photojournalism program at Boston University. I firmly believe that had I not been through the soul-searching, challenge, and success of this past year, the opportunity for the position at BU would not have come my way. I am excited and energized by this new chapter in my worklife, and I approach it with clarity of purpose and passion that would have been missing in years past.

Q: Would you give us some examples of letting go of the plan and attending to the process? For example, you mentioned that your Web site was an afterthought; yet, it has become primary marketing tool.

A: I am at my best when things are in flux. This is certainly true of my photography. I capture my strongest images when subjects are moving, events are happening. I do not "control" the action well. My set-up photos are not my strength.

I have found recently that this need to move, to react, is a metaphor for other aspects of my worklife as well. When you first suggested a Web site to me, I looked at it strictly as a backup promotional tool. As in, "You can also check out my work on the Web." But after working with a talented web designer, I discovered the site was a powerful expression of who I am and what I do for my customers. The result was that the majority of my successful leads came through my site: people I had not met or talked to, who were not referred to me but found me strictly on the strength of the photographs and writing on my site. This has been both gratifying and astonishing. Again, it was not in the original plan, but letting go of that plan and moving with what proved successful has made all the difference in my business.

Q: What do you mean by "letting your faith sink in"?

A: I have always had issues with self-confidence, and the process of this past year has gone a long way to overcome those limitations. When I talk about faith, it is about faith in myself. I put myself completely on the line this year when I started into business. The speech from the movie Apollo 13 kept coming back to me: "Failure is not an option." I had to succeed. My family was depending on me and I could not fail them. I had to have faith in myself and in what I was doing, and that faith had to come through to people who were trusting me to record some of the most important events in their lives. I knew I took good pictures, but I had to believe in my ability to build a successful business on the foundation of my photographic skills and talents. The more people [that] responded to me, the stronger my faith became and the more I was willing to depend on it. I've let my faith sink in and learned to use it. My faith gives me a positive attitude, enabling me to find learning experiences in whatever I do.

Q: What are some of the thoughts and questions that serve to guide you through the process?

A: What can I do to improve my work? How can I reach out to more people? In what ways can I deliver my message more effectively? These questions are constants, challenging me to do better every time. In my photography business, I have to remember all the time that I am doing work that is very, very important to my customers. I may be shooting dozens of events in a year, but for each of them, this is the only one that matters. It's a positive outlook, but one that accepts self-criticism. When I realize I could have done something better, it doesn't mean I didn't do a good job. It just means I can do even better the next time.

And this is going to sound very corny, but it is a very important part of my attitude: be nice to everybody. Being abrasive and pushy may work in some professions, but not in mine. I have yet to meet the person who can get under my skin or make me impatient on a job, but I can count many people who have relaxed and cooperated when confronted by a smile and friendly comment.

Q: What are you committed to, and how does your commitment act as your guide?

A: I am committed to helping people tell the stories of the most important events of their lives. I want to deliver to them a set of photographs that will capture all the emotions of their experience and bring them back [to the moment] for years to come. I am committed, quite simply, to making people happy with my work.

And now with my new responsibilities at Boston University, I am committed to educating young photojournalists in the skills they need to succeed in their chosen field, and to helping them gain entry into the profession that has given me so much satisfaction.

Q: You've said, "The results are part of the process." Would you explain?

A: As I said previously, every experience should be a learning opportunity. The results become part of the process because they inform my progress, my need to keep growing and improving. Rather than just passing along photos to my customers, I look at them very critically, finding fault and looking for the areas that need improvement. Then I step back, take some time, and look at them again, trying to see them as my customers will. I'm almost always pleased at that point but it's necessary to work through it so that I get the full benefit of the experience. This process can be applied to any experience in work and life: keep a positive attitude, but always look to improve.

Q: As most of us do, you have to work. How has attending to the process been a catalyst for you to earn a living and live a more satisfying life? Are there a few practical tips that you might share, especially ones that would help during tough times?

A: It is true, I have to work. One of the surprising lessons I learned over the past year is that if I didn't have to work, I would anyway. I found I need satisfying work to feel a connection to my community and to a significant part of myself.

Going through the process has shown me just how fortunate I am. During my darkest hours of discouragement and depression following my layoff, my family stood by me and expressed their faith in me. At no time did I feel pressure from them, only support. I am very lucky to have a wonderful marriage to an exceptional woman and two children who reaffirm my faith in life everyday. I live in a great community, with a deep network of friends. It is, indeed, a wonderful life and I give thanks every day for all the blessings I receive.

My practical tips would include accentuating the positive. Keep work in perspective; it is important, without a doubt. But it is only your work. I was lucky in that I never lost sight of what is truly vital to me: family, friends, and community. I'm hopeful that my work contributes to the life of that community in a positive way. Before I got my business up and running, I donated my time and talent, providing photography to schools, amateur theater groups, and charitable organizations. I wasn't making any money, but it felt so good to be able to give of my skill and myself to benefit others. I would advise anyone going through work crisis to try to find a way to give of themselves and their talents. It certainly helped me reconnect with my passion, and contributed to that moment of epiphany: "I'm a photographer."

Peter's *commitments* to his family and to helping people tell the stories of the most important events of their lives and his *courage and honesty* with himself and others energized and sustained his journey even through the darkest periods. Knowing what he was committed to was the fuel for his productivity. He did not act desperately but was determined to take one step, only one step, daily. Planning was simply a guidance mechanism to be altered as he tested ideas and options throughout his process.

In conclusion, the process of confronting and reframing those things that happen to us and committing to what matters can be a powerful stimulus for personal and professional growth. Learning to sit at the feet of our own lives and allowing ourselves to be taught by them can propel us toward a lifetime of success and satisfaction.

Make a Choice

Some of us are pushed into our next adventure—laid off or fired—with nowhere to go when we get up in the morning. And others, bored by their routine, make the decision to stretch themselves toward new possibilities. Both scenarios can be seen as new chapters in your life, but only if you chose.

I have chosen to play the flute—burn the grass—not knowing where it will take me. So far I've written about my playing, talked with other musicians about their experiences, tried seamlessly to slur back and forth between a D and an E, and remain continually challenged by this silver pipe that rests in a small rectangular box.

Playing the flute takes me out of the box, into living life more fully. Even though I chose it, sometimes I curse the opportunity. It's hard work to play. And this is my point: no matter how your next adventure is served you, whether it is foisted upon you or you go after it, ultimately *you're the boss.* When you've made your choice, you're committed to continue trying. If you're working "with" others, they will support your dreams just as you help them fulfill their goals. The ongoing questions are: Will you have faith in yourself? Will you have faith in the process of what you need coming to you? Will you do the hard work? If you do, I guarantee, you'll play.

Who's the Boss?
Check-In: Creating Meaningful Work

1. Will you have faith in yourself?

2. Will you have faith in the process of what you need coming to you?

3. Will you do the hard work?

4. What are you committed to?

5. What are you waiting for to make your contribution?

Bibliography

Arrien, Angeles. "The Bridge of Healing: Discovering the Universal Themes of Human Culture." Magical Blend, October 1990: 92–4.

Castaneda, Carlos. The Fire from Within. New York: Simon and Schuster, 1984.

Dudley, David; Hayward, Corinne; Hesse, Monica; Hopkins, Michael; Howard, Jennifer; Ianzito, Christina; Johnson, Marilyn; Newcott, Bill; McGanney Nolan, Abby; Pouncey, Maggie; Reed, J.D.; and Spayde, Jon. "The Fearless Fifty." AARP, March/April 2003: 57.

Hanh, Thich Nhat. Being Peace. Berkeley: Parallax Press, 1987: 6.

Handy, Charles. The Age of Unreason. Boston: Harvard Business School Press, 1989): 178.

Handy, Charles. The Hungry Spirit. New York: Broadway Books, 1998: xviii.

Hudson, Frederic M. The Adult Years. San Francisco: Jossey-Bass Publishers, 1999: 214.

Jacobsen, Mary. Hand Me Down Dreams: How Families Influence Our Career Paths. New York: Three Rivers Press, 2000: 126.

Levinson, Harry. The Great Jackass Fallacy. Cambridge: Harvard University Press, 1973: 10.

Levinson, Daniel J. The Seasons of a Man's Life. New York: Ballantine Books, 1978: 9.

Levy, Mark. Accidental Genius. San Francisco: Berrett-Koehler Publishers, 2000.

Maslow, AH. The Farther Reaches of Human Nature. New York: Viking Press, 1971: 192.

May, Rollo. The Art of Counseling. Nashville: Abingdon, 1993: 152.

Mood, John J. L. Mood, Rilke on Love and Other Difficulties. New York: (W. W. Norton & Company, 1975:), 25.

Peck, Scott M. The Road Less Traveled. New York: Simon and Schuster, 1978: 15.

Rollo, May. Man's Search for Himself. New York: W. W. Norton & Company, 1953: 21, 33.

Satir, Virginia. Peoplemaking. Palo Alto: Science and Behavior Books, 1972: 22–3.

Wheatley, Margaret. Turning to One Another. San Francisco: Berrett-Koehler Publishers, 2002: 25.

Index

About the Author

Cliff Hakim is founder of Rethinking Work®, a career and executive counseling service. He works with individuals and groups, both inside and outside of organizations. His focus is self-leadership, guiding and supporting people to take charge of their worklife.

Cliff has delivered presentations globally, from California to Connecticut and from Haiti to England, on the matter of a "self-employed" attitude. His clients have included Fortune 500 companies, Start-ups, and non-profit organizations and associations. He is the author of *When You Lose Your Job*, and publishes a newsletter devoted to his clients' purpose, passion, and productivity.

E-mail: cliff@rethinkingwork.com

Web site: www.rethinkingwork.com

About the Author